I0438356

Tim E. Davidson, Sr.

Printed in the United States of America

First Printing: December 2011

ISBN-978-1467959940

Acknowledgements

I dedicate this book to my sources of Inspiration:
Allison Davidson (my loving wife)

Ciera and Tim Jr. (my wonderful children)

Jaiden Taylor Davidson (my grandson)

Tiffany Smith (Jaiden's mother)

Minnie O. Sanders (my mother)

Buford Davidson (my father-Deceased)

Dorothy Winfield (my mother-in-law)

Gloria Williams (aunt)

Bettie O. Davis (aunt)

Edith Melton

Tullie Melton

Juanita Hilliard

Many family members and friends

Table of Contents

Introduction

During one of the more recent campaigns for the presidential nomination, a now infamous candidate ran on a platform aimed at eliminating the "two America's" that existed in our country. In today's economy it is easy to come to the conclusion that there are really two Americas. The haves and the have nots. Honestly, I wish it was that simple. In fact it is much more complicated. We have at least five economies that are alive and well in America and are becoming more and more prominent with every passing decade.

First, we have those who are one months worth of food stamps away from starving. These are the unemployed, underemployed poor people we see in the grocery stores, malls and Walmarts that dot the landscape of our country. Next, we have those who are one pay check or two away from losing everything they have worked so hard to obtain. Their day to day work routines are the only thing that keeps the food stamp rolls from expanding out of control. The third group is represented by those of us who make enough to create the appearance that they are living the American dream with a measured amount of success. These people have a handle on their budgets enough to keep their heads above water, save a little money, have decent insurance, drive decent vehicles and plan vacations they really can't afford. The fourth group is occupied by those who have issues, and occasional struggles common to man. However, their economic status makes money the least of their concerns. Finally, the fifth group is the elite of America for which money has never been and will never be a problem. They are the inventors and re-inventors of the elusive American Dream.

Unfortunately, for time immemorial African Americans and certain other minorities in America have almost exclusively resided in the first three groups and they represent a disproportionate number of those who are in groups one and two. This is of course not by accident but by design. It is a result of subsisting in a system that was never designed for them to prosper and actually promotes and perpetuates their current positions. To put it another way, the deck has been stacked against African Americans from day one and the motives and intents of the card dealers have never changed. The tragic thing is that African Americans and other similar minorities are either unaware of the situation or in some form of self-delusion that allows them to mistakenly believe that they can actually win despite 400 years of evidence to the contrary.

Right now, I know that this comes across as a bold, unpatriotic, pessimistic and even un-Godly thing to say for many who are reading this introduction. However, let me make it clear that I am a devout Christian who strongly believes that this is the greatest country on earth. Tears come to my eyes every time I hear the singing of our national anthem or any song that testifies to the greatness of this country and invokes God's blessings and prosperity. However, I simply feel that it is necessary to face and speak the truth with the utmost urgency. It is time for us to critically assess what has and is being done to suppress the economic success of minorities like the African-American community. Of course, this includes understanding not only those external factors that stand in the way. But it also requires acknowledging and addressing those internal factors that we have allowed to "keep us down."

Now this book would not be worth the paper on which it is written or the code created to make it digital, if we did not suggest a path to a better tomorrow for the African American community and other minorities that find themselves in similar circumstances. Therefore, I will spend the bulk of this book sharing what I believe are the true circumstances that African-Americans face. I will add to that my diagnosis of the problems we cause for ourselves as we attempt to reach fulfillment on the promise of America. Then, I will propose solutions that are intended to move these groups from a state of feigned prosperity to realistic economic achievement on their own terms.

To that end, I will introduce several situations that represent what many groups of individuals dwelling in the environment called the US economy face everyday. The hope is that you will be able to quickly identify with these not so fictional situations and curiously follow along as I share how they can survive in this harsh, unrelenting environment. Finally, I invite you to relax, open your mind and envision how your life can be drastically different than you have ever imagined.

Section 1

Chapter 1- The Desert Land

I can assume that you, like me and most others have not spent much time in a barren desert-like environment. However, it is not hard to imagine the fundamental challenges to human life that is presented by deserts like the Sahara, Mojave and those present in places like Somalia and Darfur. These scorched, dry and lifeless places do not offer their unfortunate inhabitants or visitors much chance of a prosperous existence. In fact, mere survival is a 50-50 proposition at best and death after any long term residency could be viewed as a blessing. The Christian Bible conveys the point that "Days of Man are few and those are full of trouble." In no circumstance is this more evident than in the lives of those who live in the desert regions of God's "green" earth.

A few years ago, a well known and now deceased comic used those suffering in the drought stricken regions of Africa as the center of one of his often repeated jokes. In paraphrasing his joke, he mocked the Africans by asking, "Do you want to know why you are dying, hungry and thirsty..? YOU ARE LIVING IN A DESERT!!!!. Whether you laughed at the joke or thought it was insensitive and crude, the point he was trying to make is real and worth considering. Why would you choose to live in an environment that was harsh, cruel, uninviting and the main source of your frustration, pain and suffering? Wouldn't you at least attempt to move, escape or encourage your offspring to do what hasn't been possible for you?

The answers to these questions do not come easily and keeps many scratching their heads in astonishment or turning their nose up in disbelief.

In a similarly amazing situation, their are millions of people who live in barren, impoverished societies and embrace religious beliefs and taboos that cause thousands to die of starvation and live in abject poverty year after year. To some, it is fairly absurd to keep a beast like an ox alive and allow your children to starve to death because your religion regards the beast as sacred and untouchable. Again, the questions do not lend themselves to easy answers. Nonetheless, the consequences and results are the same. The harshness of the environment and a refusal to accept/adopt a different way of thinking brings about self-inflicted destruction. The bottom line is that the deserts are no place to be for anyone who wants to thrive and the restrictive thinking that keeps people there are sealing their fate.

It nearly brings tears to my eyes to witness a similar scenario playing out in the lives of African-Americans and other minorities in the economic climate that prevails in America. Sure, the weather in America is rarely a factor and life of some sorts is almost a guarantee. However, just like the mirage that raises the hopes of a deadly thirsty man, the mirage of economic prosperity deceives the vulnerable into believing that their watershed moment is only a few moments away. Why can't they see it? Why are they so sure that they can obtain success? Why do they convey such hope to their children generation after generation? Why do they wind up blaming themselves for not reaching the mountain top? Why do they make choices that are intended to improve their condition but the results are just the opposite? As difficult as it may seem, let's attempt to answer these questions. Not because I am confident of the answers, but it is unacceptable to leave these questions unanswered.

But first we must talk about the harsh economic climate in which they suffer everyday. And here is where we run into a major hurdle because describing the economic client is like painting a picture of the wind. You can't convey an impression of the wind without speaking of its impact, what it is affecting. Therefore, I must take the same approach.

Chapter 2 - Income...

Let's start with the simple concept of annual income from work or other occupational activities. On average, an African-American earns 35 percent less than the majority group. Since, the average income of the majority group is $72,000. This means that the African-American wage earner has 22,000 fewer dollars at his disposal each year and over a 40 year career that adds up to $880,000. If they were able to make, save and invest 10% of this difference at a rate of return of just 10% that would mean an additional $1.13 million in net worth for a total of $2,000,000 in earnings and savings.

But, the story gets even worse when you consider the fact that the majority group reaches this income level as much as 10 years sooner! (If you have the stomach for it, see the staggering figures in the the chapters that follow). It gets down right depressing when you account for the fact that African-Americans lose as much as five years of income because of shorter life expectancy. Also, the income of the African-American male is significantly lower than his female counterpart, who appears to have an easier time navigating the corporate ladder. I think it is unfruitful to ponder reasons for this disparity because just like the devastating heat of the sun, simply talking about it will not stop it from occurring.

Since this pattern is not a new concept, generations of disparity have led to even a gloomier picture. Individuals in the majority group not only can count on higher salaries, they can depend on much more financial support from their parents, siblings, grandparents, uncles, aunts, cousins, family friends, etc, etc. This treasure trove of support not only gets them off to a much faster start, but helps them avoid mountains of debt that cripples every one else. The result is prefunded college educations, significant down payments on homes, yearly vacations, better credit scores, larger retirement accounts, fewer bills and the list could go on for days.

It is also worth mentioning the greased skids that exist for the majority group when it comes to employment. Affluent friends and family in high places leads to near guaranteed employment when compared to the job struggles of African Americans. You could argue that affirmative action levels the playing field, but that argument will not hold water. Especially, when you consider that some believe it is easier for an ex-con from the majority group to get a job than most minorities with a college education. To make it clear, I am in support of affirmative action but do not see it as some sort of panacea or silver bullet. You cannot legislate your way to equality in economic conditions any more than you can create laws that improve morality.

Chapter 3 - Cost of Credit

From credit cards to mortgages to auto loans, by every measure, African-Americans and other minorities are saddled with higher rates of interest, fees and penalties for borrowing money to purchase the things they need or want. You need only to search the internet or review financial literature to collect mountains of evidence that supports this position. Some credit card companies, with the support of an admittedly flawed credit reporting and rating system, impose stiff unconscionable rates with low credit limits to millions of African-Americans everyday. These shackles lead to a perpetual state of debt and low credit ratings. Low credit ratings lead to higher rates, lower levels of credit and quick defaults. This never ending cycle persists generation after generation because somehow African-Americans have convinced themselves (or have been convinced) that it is all due to poor money management and lack of initiative on their part.

Let me illustrate this in a simple example. An African-American with modest income and a decent but short credit history will typically receive a credit limit not exceeding $1000 at the standard rate of 19.99% or higher. On the other hand, a comparably situated majority group member will be given the benefit of the doubt and receives a $5000 or higher credit limit with a significantly better rate. Here's where things get very interesting. The African-American may need to use the card to make Christmas special and purchases at least $750 but not more than the $1000 credit limit for presents. The majority member purchases items for Christmas that total $2500, more than 3 times the amount spent by the minority card holder. Both pay their payment on time but neither one of them pays off the balance within the grace period (although the majority member is much more likely to have the resources to do so).

The surprising result is that the African-American will take a significant hit on their credit score while the majority member adds a positive impact on their credit rating. The difference is caused by the low credit line and the fact that in one instance 70% of the credit line is used. If the African-American pays his minimum payments on time month after month, it will take some time for him to get the remaining balance below 70%. Until he does, his credit score stays down. Now suppose the African- American is able and unwisely gets four other cards with similarly low credit lines to match buying power and to support his family's buying needs. If you think this is unrealistic, please note that more than one well known credit card company has used this strategy to build their market share for years! As each of these cards exceed the 70% mark, the credit score declines accordingly. So you have one with five cards, $2500 in debt with a horrible credit score and no chance at getting a decent rate on a car or home. The other winds up with the same amount of debt and positioning themselves for a good rate on the house or car they have had their eyes on for months!

In order to play the game and win in the current system, the ability to obtain credit and maintaining a good credit rating is essential. This is not only true for African- American adults, but for their children and grand children that follow. While others are helping their children get off to a good start because they are "valid" co-signers on loans or can use their credit to supply the funds that help them pursue their dreams, most African-Americans can only struggle to keep their heads above water.

Chapter 4- Pursuing the American Dream

When it comes to "owning a piece of the American Dream", it has been well documented that African-Americans have received the proverbial "short end of the stick" for years. The tactics of red-lining certain neighbors, targeting certain groups with non-beneficial loan products, and limiting the use of home equity has historically been a common practice in the mortgage and home loan industries. And, there is no real indication that the practice has been abandoned. The list of villains in this space includes everyone from banks of all sizes, shady financial institutions, real estate agents, mortgage brokers, real estate assessors, mortgage insurers and even the local and federal government. At every step of the journey to and through home ownership the African-American faces a perilous and often unprofitable experience.

It begins with well-intentioned but often misguided agents who steer them to less than desirable neighborhoods and fail to live up to the full extent of their certification by keeping vulnerable clients from bad loan deals. Their goal has been to close a deal as soon as possible with maximum agency profit regardless of the impact it has on the buyer and seller. According to their ads, it's always a good time to buy and sell. This is not because there are great deals available or you can get the maximum for your home, but they need the money to stay in business! You can argue that this is not just a minority issue, but it is hard to dismiss the point that the strategy is much more effective against those who are desperate to become home owners and minorities represent a disproportionate percentage of that group.

Shady and unconscionable financial services firms (who nowadays often double as the home builder/developer through corporate partnerships to keep the profits in house) lay in wait for vulnerable would be homeowners. Again, they are usually indiscriminating, but do take advantage of government programs aimed at minority home ownership and these under educated and unsuspecting consumers to sell overpriced homes using questionable to downright criminal loan approval practices after getting them to invest a sizable down payment and sign an iron-clad contract. To make matters worse, they funnel business to more than appreciative assessors who make sure that the loan is always 'workable.'

While the rise of independent mortgage brokers has made the path to homeownership more accessible, it has also made it infinitely more treacherous for the vulnerable. These modern day 'desert marauders' systematically and shamelessly ambush loan seekers and rob them of their hard earned money through excessive fees, unnecessarily high interest rates and mortgage insurance premiums. Using morally suspect practices many of these mortgage brokers have become millionaires from the comfort of their living room couches! Now that the housing bubble has burst and their victims now face foreclosure, they have moved on to use their new found wealth to purchase these distressed homes at a fraction of their value via foreclosure or short sales. The results are 'house poor' homeowners or debt-laden former homeowners wondering whether the pursuit of the American Dream was worth the pain and suffering.

I slightly hinted at the role that government has played in this continuing travesty of justice. Let's get more specific. It starts with the well intentioned but under-regulated efforts to make ownership a realty for many more African-Americans. These programs make it very attractive and lucrative to pursue minority home-seekers and help them secure mortgages. However, the lack of rules opened the flood gates for the corrupting power of money to blind the judgment of large firms as well as budding entrepreneurs. The government also did not have the foresight to understand how big banks will help out by allowing the brokers and mortgage companies to transfer the risk to others thus making room for more risky loans. Allowing such practices as stated income loans, split loans, unrealistic adjustable mortgages, vertical supply chains, and binding contracts not subject to loan approvals increased the heat of the 'desert' to near intolerable levels while creating a nearly irresistible mirage of promised prosperity.

Now many may argue that all groups have been equally targeted and negatively impacted by these tactics. The validity of such an argument would be hard to dispute on its face. But, a deeper assessment that considers extenuating and contributing factors brings into focus the compounded impact to the African-American consumer. Factors such as marginal credit, minimal resources, age at time of purchase, employment instability, and little to no support makes the implications of a faulty home buying decision a 'dream-killing' and financial devastating event. Most of the African-Americans who have been caught in the trap will never recover to the point where home ownership is again a viable option. These people will live the rest of their lives silently wondering if it was ever worth the effort. You can only imagine the advice they will give their children or grand children. And for those yet to pursue or attain home ownership, the recent debacles in the mortgage industry have made the journey infinitely more challenging. As a result, all of the gains achieved by African-Americans will be wiped out by the turn of the next decade.

Chapter 5 - Getting Behind the Wheel

Everyone depends on access to reliable transportation to reach their desired destinations be it work, home, the babysitters or the hospital. However, what that 'ride' costs you is highly dependent on your credit and others' subjective opinions of what you can or will pay for the wheels. These 'factors' almost always work against the African-American whose needs always outpace available funds. Unfortunately car dealerships, banks, credit unions, auto finance companies and auto insurance companies have made these factors the cornerstones of their business models. This is another place where the disparity in income and credit status significantly impacts the "customer experience" of African-Americans.

Because of income restrictions, African-Americans have to attain lower quality or older vehicles. These vehicles don't last as long, have higher maintenance cost and offer a lower level of safety. They are also pushed to second tier dealerships or used car lots where quality and reliability is even more suspect. Upon entering these places, an assessment of your financial condition has already been made. Dealers create deals with finance companies and pad the rates resulting in a substantial kick back for the dealer that the buyer will pay for over time. As a result, African-Americans are much more likely to leave the dealership driving some type of vehicle but also having a much higher interest rate, payment and financing period than expected or warranted. In many instances, African-Americans are offered rates exceeding 30% when they should be able to qualify for something significantly lower.

Once purchased, the vehicle has to be insured and the pain intensifies. Many insurance agencies unfairly use credit ratings to establish rates and this leads to artificially high insurance rates, large down payments and inflexible payment terms. This results in a higher overall monthly obligation. This is even more critical when there are young drivers involved. You may have never thought of this, but many of the rates applied to young drivers are based on the driving performance of children in the majority group. African-American teens may get stopped more often for other reasons but get traffic tickets and are involved in accidents at a much lower rate. This is astonishing when you understand that most African-Americans cannot afford to give their children cars during their teenage years. However, when they do the rates imposed on the majority teens are applied to them.

If the average car costs $12,000, the African-American would pay over $2000 in additional interest, insurance and maintenance over the life of the car due to these seemingly innocuous differences in economics. Since the average person may have seven cars during their lifetime. This could add up to a $15,000 deficit in wealth accumulation!

Chapter 6 - Insurance: Owning a piece of the rock

As a little boy, living in the "projects" of downtown Newport News, I witnessed things that I now understand were occurring all over the country in neighborhoods like mine. Every Saturday, my parents and the other adults living in the housing project known as Marshall Courts, were awakened to doorbell rings from 'traveling' salesmen. These Saturday morning invaders were selling everything from encyclopedias to burial plots. The most prolific of the offerings peddled by these suited gypsies was some form of insurance. For a few bucks a month my parents and others were promised the security of life, death and burial insurances. These policies guaranteed peace and security when difficult moments arise. Of course, these policies typically turned out to be full of false promises and guaranteed nothing but broken dreams.

These bait and switch policies were often difficult to read and even harder to understand. People with limited educations were left to figure out actuarial tables, confusing payout scenarios, diminishing valuation tables, loan payback schedules and complicated policy cancellation procedures. They also were suckered into purchasing insurance instruments that cost them far more than they would get out of the policies even in the best of circumstances.

Too many times, these people would have to purchase policy after policy because of the worst practice of all, quick cancellations due to non-receipt of payment. As written, these policies mandated on-time payments with no margin for error. If the insured missed a payment by one day, the policy was deemed null and void. Too many times, people have lost coverage and everything they had invested in it because the payment was considered late or somehow didn't get applied to their account and they were never warned. Their only recourse was to start all over again with a new policy.

I acknowledge that some of you have never heard of things like this and may be skeptical. So let me share with you how it typically occurs. A middle- aged, elderly African-American who has not been able to save for the future because they have spent all of their lives struggling to make ends meet, is approached with an opportunity to ensure that their final expenses are paid for so that they will not be a burden on their children. They also are told that with a small monthly premium that will 'never' go up, they can help their children have a better life than they have endured. From their vantage point, these two promises are hard to resist.

The hopeful customer makes a decision to purchase the policy believing that it is worth making the sacrifice to pay the monthly premiums. They typically do not have anyone to help them read and understand the fine print. After all, this guy seems trustworthy enough and they wouldn't be selling a bad product because the "government" would not allow it! One to ten years down the road, when the policy premiums double because of "premium shortfalls" or some other extenuating circumstances, the customer is struggling to make the payments. As soon as they miss a payment or can no longer afford the policy, a cancellation notice arrives in the mail and they are offered another replacement policy that is magically better than the one they had.

Needless to say, the agents were fully aware of the potential for default and actually banked on it occurring because these amounted to easy profits and recurring commissions. They would never have to find new feeding grounds because of a never ending supply of vulnerable and naïve clients. It is hard to fathom the countless millions in unfruitful premiums that have poured out of these communities through unfair and deceptive practices. I often wonder how such individuals could sleep at night when they know how they have 'robbed" the elderly, many of whom are on fixed or minimal incomes.

I wish I could say that these practices are a thing of the past. However, the only thing that is in the past is the mode of operation and the players in the game. Junk Mail and slick television, radio, and internet advertising on every conceivable channel with African-American patronage bombard the airways in place of the Saturday morning ritual. And now, shadow companies leverage African-Americans looking to make it rich to make the pitch for them. The result is an ever-growing and lucrative enterprise that continues to get its full off of these communities from one generation to the next. It is hard to contemplate the millions of dollars in premiums that have and continue to flow out of these communities. Funds that could be used to establish savings accounts, defer the cost of school, to pay for reliable transportation or needed medical treatment just to name a few.

Chapter 7 - Investing/Saving

It should not come as a surprise to anyone that African-Americans lag way behind their cultural contemporaries in investing and the use of interest bearing financial products that can lead to a stronger economic future. Although the reasons for this are many, only a few have gotten much press in the centuries since slavery was abolished. The most prominent are those that depict African-Americans as unsophisticated, uneducated and uncontrolled squanderers of wealth. If you believed everything that has been published, reported or implied, African-Americans would rather spend every dime they had instead of saving a single penny. The reasons these views have longevity is due to the fact that there are all seasoned with small pellets of truth. I explain these fragments of truth in the chapter of the book called "Self-Inflicted Wounds". However, these reasons are only superficial and are intended to cover up the realities associated with "systemically driven" poverty and structured "financial captivity".

To understand the impact of this segment of the American Economy, we need to bring to the fore the under lying principles and assumptions that support our financial system. First is the fact that in order to invest and save you need to have funds available to invest and to set aside. These funds are typically above that which is needed to support your day to day life or at least can be replaced by something else like resources made available through some sort of support structure. If you do set aside funds that are needed for the day to day without replacement, you either do not survive or have to use the funds before any real value can be gained from setting it aside. An illustration is in order at this point.

Cheetahs are some of the most majestic creatures on earth. I have always been impressed with their sleekness, speed and agility. However, the very attributes that draws my attention are the things that make their lives so vulnerable to individual extinction. These animals are always in a delicate balance between thriving and dying because of what it takes to find and obtain sustenance. It takes so much energy and effort to patiently and aggressively pursue and capture their next meal that a slight miscalculation, mistake or unsuspecting rival can lead to premature death. Considering this situation, it may seem logical for the cheetah to set aside and store up food for the times when a meal is not available. However, for these animals, meals come so far apart that they and their offspring must consume their meal almost immediately to renew and restore their depleted bodies. In fact, more often than not, the adult cheetah must deny her own hunger to ensure that her young are able to eat enough to survive.

But let us suppose that the cheetah decides to do something different than what her instincts are telling her to do. She decides that instead of devouring all of the antelope she has just killed, she will find a good hiding place and store up a portion of the carcass for a future meal. First, every time she has a struggle with capturing the next meal for herself or her offspring, she will be tempted to go dig up that stored meal to quiet the calls of hunger. The temptation will be magnified by every hunger pain felt or every whine from the offspring requesting something to eat. In fact, her instinct to meet the need of her offspring will be nearly irresistible! Ironically, when she does give in to the temptation and returns to partake of that stored meal, she finds that the meal has been partially or completely devoured by bugs, worms, rats, vultures, hyenas, wild dogs, lions, another cheetah, etc, etc!!

Like the cheetah, many people in America live on the edge of extinction and rely on their meager earnings or resources to make it from day to day. So many others have over extended the ability of their resources and are for all practical purposes in the same situation. As a result, they are living from paycheck to paycheck, refund to refund and don't see a clear path to living any other way. To them, setting aside funds for tomorrow that are needed to meet the demands of 'today' are an exercise in futility. Every struggle they have will lead them to consider tapping into any shallow reserves at their disposal to fill the gap or stay afloat. Afterwards, they rededicate themselves to saving only to continue the cycle a short time later. Each turn of this cycle puts them further and further behind because of the time value of money and the cost of tapping into savings prematurely. This is where the nature of our economic system makes matters worse.

In America, the more you have the cheaper it is to enjoy the benefits of our financial system. Financial institutions offering investing and saving products apply nearly all of their fees on those who can least afford them. These fees, penalties, charges, threshold limits, etc act just like those bugs, vultures and other wild beast that eat away at the "stored meal". Unless you have thousands of dollars to leave in a bank for an extended period of time, you will not be able to avoid being charged monthly fees that erode or negate any interest savings you expect to receive. If you can't avoid tapping into retirement savings to avoid financial calamity, you face substantial tax implications and financial penalties that set you back for years. These "rules" that were intended to encourage saving for retirement often leaves many people worse off than ever when retirement time does come.

Chapter 8 - Education

We have been often told that education is a priceless and irrevocable treasure. Others have touted education as the only real path to a better life both socially and financially. Therefore, any level of education attainment is considered worth the time and investment. In today's environment a high school education is nothing more than a must and multiple college degrees are becoming the standard. To that end, countless resources have been and continue to be poured into our education system to ensure every child has an equal chance at a 'good' education. Also, traditional and on-line schools are expanding or popping up in every place imaginable to take advantage of the enormous push for advanced education.

These new bastions of education promise quicker and more convenient paths to that all important diploma. Their tremendous financial success is made possible by the huge void generated by traditional education tracks that have either underperformed or denied education to millions across this country. Our primary and secondary education system is rife with inefficiencies and pitfalls that leave many African Americans barely prepared for minimum wage jobs. The poor-level of preparation for these groups make success in traditional colleges and universities a tenable proposition at best. Overcoming the initial barriers of standardized tests and historical preferences to acceptance has led to the poor representation at "top echelon" schools and a struggle for limited spaces at the rest.

To their credit, certain schools have open door policies that allow academically unprepared students a chance to "prove their metal" on a trial basis. These colleges have traditionally been historically black colleges and universities that are sprinkled across most of our country. However, the value of these degrees in corporate America are still very much in doubt. Even more troubling is the fact that there isn't even a debate about the relative value of these degrees versus the degrees from "mainstream" schools.

The officials at HBCUs love to brag about their tradition of providing affordable education for many who would not have otherwise had the opportunity. It is extremely hard to argue with that fact. Each year thousands of Africa-Americans, who otherwise would be labeled as unfit for most public and private four year schools, check in to crowded, aging dorms at these historically significant landmarks. However, these same officials rarely call out or brag about their retention, graduation and placement rates.

One familiar HBCU in Virginia unceremoniously holds a graduation rate of 39% and a first year retention rate that is not much better. This means that 61% of their students leave school not holding a diploma but only holding significant student loan debt that will become an albatross around their necks weighing them down for the rest of their lives. You could argue that most students carry some type of student loan debt and hence all have to carry a similar burden. But you would be forgetting the disparity in income potential and financial support between the groups to manage that debt.

If HBCUs do boast about their academic success, it is normally in the form of cleverly crafted statements that shed the best light on what would normally be a very bleak picture. HBCU deans, chancellors, chief of staff, etc, like to keep the attention on one or two programs for which they have achieved a measurable amount of success. For instance, a well known HBCU on the east coast touts their continued success in graduating and finding work for a handful of pharmacy students with doctoral level degrees. And use this success as justification for charging Ivy League rates for in-state and out-of state tuition. However, they never mention their inability to gain prominence or respect for any of their other programs. In fact, the majority of their graduates struggle to find employment in the field of choice or find themselves grossly under-employed for most of their careers. If the parchment they receive at these schools after graduation where currency, they would be worth 50 cents to the dollar.

I happened to attend a local city council meeting several years ago. During the meeting the topic of teacher starting salaries for the district was the highlight of the night. Some of the teachers were upset that the new hires from the local HBCU were systematically given lower starting salaries than their counterparts who had graduated from mainstream universities in the area. The startling part of the conversation came when a prominent female on the council clearly and without revocation stated the following; "You cannot begin to compare the teaching degrees from these schools [HBCUs] with that of Christopher Newport and similar schools." Her clear message was that in her opinion these students did not measure up and therefore do not deserve equal pay and treatment.

If this was an isolated event or the rantings of one out of touch person this would not be a big deal. Unfortunately, this is the norm and not the exception that perpetuates the pay disparity, reluctance to hire and huge differences in promotions. Most HBCUs only have a few companies willing to actively recruit their students. In fact, the deans at these schools have taken one of two very odd strategies that make it even tougher for their students. The first is a sought of begging strategy where they peddle their students to whomever shows up at their door. They don't care what type of job their students get; they just want to be able to say that a majority of their students find employment after college. They never challenge these companies to provide compatible positions and salaries. Also, the schools never follow-up to determine whether their graduates are thriving in the companies that offer them jobs.

As a result, many college-educated and degreed African-Americans are working in positions that really don't require a degree! Don't believe me? Take a tour of your local bank, call center, pharmacy, Wal-Mart, department store, fast food chain, rental car agency and package delivery company. These places are filled with once promising college grads seeking to leverage their hard earned degrees from HBCUs and mainstream universities. There are even many more who have given up on finding a job and return to school to get more of this 'invaluable' education!

The second strategy is akin to "pimping out' their students to the highest bidder. These officials make no bones about the entry fees and commitment levels for accessing their students. Companies willing to pay for the privilege, get near exclusive access to the best students. This works out pretty well for the best and the brightest because they get to work for great companies and obtain very good competitive salaries. However, because so few companies get access the remaining students are left to fend for themselves in a job market that deems their diploma as second rate. The graduates who are fortunate enough to find work, also find themselves in jobs that are misaligned with their career goals or leave them wanting for equal compensation.

Of course, the promise of a good and equal education for all in practical application is a fairly new concept. I say this because of the massive resistance offered for decades by powerful forces in this country and the continued subversive efforts (e.g. "no child left behind" and the dreaded Standards of Learning testing) that have, in effect, kept educational progress in neutral for many under-privileged groups. Unfortunately, African-Americans and similar groups are the most impacted by these destructive and ultimately self-defeating practices. Since their inception little if any progress have been made in improved test scores, graduation rates and drop out rates. However, the news on the "new" standards has not all been bad. They have also served to expose many inadequate and corrupt school systems where cheating or social promotion is the rule of the day. All of the so called incentives and threats of repercussions have essentially failed or provoked unintended consequences. And, the big losers are the students who are left even more poorly prepared than they were before. As a result, the most vulnerable and resource-deprived members of our society are forced to face this vast wasteland, intellectually dehydrated with not one drop of academic achievement to quench their thirst for success in our society. I know this may come across to the underexposed mind as overstated and a bit melodramatic. However, when you realize that the government already expects a certain number of their 8 year olds will need reservations in the local penitentiary instead of college dorm rooms indicates where our societies true hopes for these children resides.

Chapter 9 - Self-inflicted wounds

It is entirely one thing to face nearly overwhelming odds against your success doing everything in your power to get out of your own way. However, it is a totally different thing to weaken your odds by doing things that make matters infinitely worse. Imagine a football team driving for the end zone and after every successful play that gains significant yards loses focus and does something that results in a negating penalty. That team is not only missing out on an opportunity to win the game, but is indicating to their opponent and the fans that they do not have what it takes to be successful. In fact, the team they are competing against gains more and more confidence in their ability to dominate with every passing mistake. Likewise, the fans will begin to berate them for their lack of discipline and lose confidence in their ability as a team.

In this section, I want to explore how African-Americans have in many ways become their own worse enemy by making crucial mistakes in an environment where they can least afford costly errors. Of course, this is not intended to pile on and vilify African-Americans for destructive behaviors. I am fully aware that all groups in America have vices that tend to lead to negative economic impacts. However, since minorities typically have minimal resources when compared to other groups, they are least able to afford wasting any of them due to false dreams, misinformation, greed, pride and self-delusion. The white American who mistakenly believes he can afford a boat or club membership has a much better chance of selling his way out of a bad deal than an African-American who believes he can afford a "brand new" Lexus.

The dirty secret behind Capitalism is that it is based on the premise that most people will never "figure it out" financially. Capitalism thrives when "the haves" are able to continually take advantage of the "have nots". When you hear political action groups talking about "wanting their America back" they are speaking of the economic conditions that allow them and them only to thrive. They are vehemently against any form of wealth re-distribution or any efforts to improve the situation of the under-privileged. How they obtained and maintain their wealth is of no consequence to them as long as they are not on the short end of the stick. Ironically, they are the first to cry foul when they become victims of the very schemes they perpetrate on others. We need only look at the victims of the Enron, WorldCom, AIG, and the Madoff scandals for evidence of their hypocrisy.

In the most basic terms possible, the engine of Capitalism is fueled by the rapid cycling of money through our economy. The faster money moves through, the better profits are for producers and investors. But the rapid cycling of money is not a natural human tendency. People are hard-wired to hoard or hold on to the things they have including money. Therefore, ever more sophisticated marketing schemes and technological advances have been developed to "intellectually and emotionally" pry these earned and unearned dollars out the hands, pockets and/or accounts of fellow capitalists.

The foundation of every marketing campaign for any product from burgers to BMWs, from jack rocks to jeans, from hobby horses to homes is to get individuals to buy more and buy it now. All commercials, infomercials, brochures, billboards, pop-up boxes, web tags, etc. are all intended to influence your subconscious to override your God-given wisdom of "I can live without it" and replace it with "I need it now!" And, by all accounts it has worked with an unsurpassed vigor that has resulted in America becoming the most prosperous and powerful nation on earth. Many would proudly proclaim that our success is due to some merited or unmerited favor from our Creator. In other words, we have been destined to lead the world and show all other nations what he requires for them to be successful.

Likewise, technology has aided in the ascendency of our nation to the elite status it now holds. The discovery of inventions like electricity, telephones, television and the rapid expansion of computing power and tools like the internet have been the catalyst for the astronomical expansion of our economy. We now have very effective tools for peddling to our citizens an endless variety of products and services that they are now convinced they can't live without. The interesting power of the marketing techniques and the technology that supports them is the fact that it works best on the deprived and underprivileged. They are more likely to "buy in to the hype with little question or reservation.

This undoubtedly permeates through every facet of our society. But, in what ways has it most manifested in the African- American community? How has it been most detrimental to the economic well being of the African-American society? What lies have been believed or perpetuated that keeps African-Americans from rising from centuries of financial oppression? Again, I don't have all of the answers but some very revealing things may be powerful clues to how we are making things harder on ourselves from generation to generation.

Chapter 10 - A High Roller Mentality on a Ghetto Budget - Lottery/Gambling

I recently came across an article that describes current research on the economic impact of the lottery on African-Americans. This article caught my attention because it painted such a sinister picture of the lottery and the devastation that it is causing in poor African-American neighborhoods. The article explained that the researchers looked at the lottery spending habits of the inhabitants in several zip codes in Chicago.

These zip codes were chosen based on their racial makeup to determine how much money was spent by various racial groups in an attempt to win the various jackpots and prizes. Several of the "black" zip codes were over 95% African- American. Likewise, the "white" zip codes predominantly consisted of Caucasians. However, the overall demographic makeup of the population mirrored those typically found in America. The researchers also wanted to know if the amount of money spent resulted in a proportional amount of money won by the various groups. The results were nothing less than astonishing. But before we reveal the results, it is worth visiting the history of the "lottery" in the African-American community.

Since African-American were "free" in this country to make their own decisions regarding their social norms, games similar to the lottery have been prevalent in African-American communities. As early as the age of five, I could remember my parents, relatives and neighbors talking about "playing the numbers". This would usually entail making a trip to a local store or a well-known home and putting a few hard-earned or not so hard earned dollars on a number that they believed would pay off big. I would often hear adult relatives, neighbors and friends speak about numbers that they had dreamed, couldn't get out of their heads or saw on license plates and were confident that they would be a winner someday. Of course, this unfounded optimism would compel them to play their numbers at every opportunity possible to "increase" their chances of winning. God forbid if their numbers hit at a time when they did not play them! This compulsion often leads to ill-advised attempts to win by using money that was needed to pay bills and purchase groceries.

These highly illegal games were just the tip of the iceberg for gambling activities that have become an "ugly" part of the fabric of the African-American culture. Their insidious impact on African-American communities rivals drugs, alcohol and violence in its devastating economic impact. Countless millions of dollars in wealth have flowed out of these communities because of greed and false hope.

Believe me when I say that the illegal "playing the numbers" has not vanished. But, it has taken back seat to two other "legal" numbers running schemes. They now come in the form of casinos and the State Lottery. Instead of going into the local grocery or backdoor of the local shot house, they enter the local convenient stores, and regional grocery stores or get on chartered buses for a day trip to the nearest casino. The peddlers of these games of chance are no longer some criminal trying to stay under the police's radar, but they are the companies and casinos sanctioned by the state! Now, the government has a vested interest in the success and viability of these games of chance. Tax revenues, state projects and public school budgets are highly dependent on the proceeds from these scourges of our society.

Of course, you may be wondering what is so bad about taking a chance on trying to improve your economic situation when you really don't have any other way of gaining the wealth you desire. You may also ask why I am attacking what most view as cheap forms of entertainment. Aren't these victimless and harmless forms of entertainment? Doesn't everyone who plays the game know what they are getting into and what they are sacrificing?

These are indeed valid questions that demand reasonable answers. First, this is not a cheap form of entertainment. The revenues generated from lotteries alone could support many small countries across the world. Second, they are highly addictive behaviors that wreck families and destroy the futures of millions. Third, they are inherently unfair to the individuals that play them the most.

Consider the results from Chicago. When the researchers compared the zip codes they discovered that nearly 60% of the money played in the Chicago-Based lottery was tendered by African-Americans. The group with the least amount of resources contributed the largest to the jackpots, promotional expenses and tax revenues generated by these "games of chance." The logical thing to deduce is that they would also receive the "lion's share" of the winnings applied to the various jackpots and prizes, The fact is you would be wrong if you conservatively guessed that they would win half of the jackpot money. You would also be in error if you assumed that they won an amount that was proportional to their overall percentage of the population that played the games.

Astonishingly, the African-Americans playing the games received less than 1 percent of the winnings! That's right I said less than 1 percent of the winnings. If this seems statistically impossible to you then we are mentally on the same planet. Since, reading these results, I have tried to rationalize how this could be statistically possible and I am still stumped. The only logical explanations I can come up with is that somebody is cooking the books, using algorithms to predict where to send the most likely winners or placing the winning scratchers in strategic locations that make it more favorable for white Americans to win. Ironically, I have not seen this question addressed by any of the brilliant minds in the fields of economics and statistics. All I can say about this matter is the same thing that my pastor would often say during his sermons: "There is a dead cat on the line some where!"

The lottery industry has also spawned very lucrative business models in books, magazines and websites that feed the "unfounded optimism" of lottery players by offering potential winning numbers or strategies to improve abysmal odds. The ironic thing is that most of the individuals buying these products do not have even the most basic understanding of statistical probabilities. Therefore, they are shelling out even more money on advice that cannot be proven to be any better than their own. And you probably guessed that many of the people purchasing these goods are minorities. (sad face)

Food For Thought:

"On July 29, 1998 the 20 state Power Ball lottery gave away a record $250,000,000 or a quarter of a billion dollars. The odds of winning are around 80 million to 1 per ticket. Even if you decide to take it in a lump sum, it is worth $130 million. Such gigantic sums of money are tempting lots of people. People are using their rent checks and paychecks to buy hundreds of tickets in an attempt to better their odds. Sure every dollar you spend increases your chances of winning, but each increase is minor. Spending $2 increases your chances from 80 million:1 to 40 million:1. Yeah you doubled your chances, but as we learned in elementary school 2 times 0 is 0, so it follows that 2 times almost 0 is also almost 0."
This valuable information was extracted from the following site:
http://members.cox.net/mathmistakes/rawdata.htm

Chapter 11 - Addicted to the Bling - Clothing, Jewelry and other Major Purchases

One of the most fascinating things I have discovered about the financial oppressed is their seemingly irresistible need to be seen and heard. It has manifested itself in many ways thru the years. Ever since some of these groups have been able to earn money, what they purchase appears to always have to make a statement to the world. This can be seen in everything from "the Sunday best' clothing, hair decorations, jewelry, designer clothing and name brand shoes. Even in the poorest neighborhoods to be able to own certain items has almost become more essential than food or shelter.

During my childhood, I vividly remember the teasing that many would have to endure because they didn't have a pair of the latest and most popular jeans. I can recall household conversations that centered on what shoes we could get for the new school year. Buying and wearing the bargain "K-Mart specials" was an open invitation for criticism and ridicule from anyone that had even an old pair of Converse sneakers. The prevailing mantra was "Don't get the ones that slip and slide, get the ones with the star on the side." Likewise, wearing cheap jeans from Roses instead of name brands like Jordache was the quickest way to remain out of the "social elite" in our neighborhood. Moreover, what came from under your Christmas Tree and out onto the streets after December 25th cemented or demolished your reputation as the trendsetters among your peers.

Now, this would be considered typical behavior if I was describing what goes on in middle income or affluent neighborhoods. However, much of this was happening while I was living in the projects of Newport News. All of these "social climbers" were equally poor and destitute with many living in subsidized housing and receiving food stamp vouchers to feed their families. To be fair this type of class distinction happens at every level of our society, but it is a sinister and devastating reality in poor communities because the negative and lasting impact on the financial well-being of the communities is enormous.

In many poor communities it is common to see children not yet able to walk outfitted with the newest pair of Jordans. These same children are dressed with expensive name brand clothing that is easily soiled by the baby food or what may leak out of the diapers they still need. This fascination with the expensive clothing is started early and continues for most thru the rest of their lives and past down to the next generation. Teenagers would rather catch pneumonia than be caught wearing a warming pleather (imitation leather) coat when they can't afford to get the 'genuine' leather. Women will spend every dime they have purchasing a Coach purse just to win the praise of their girlfriend. Teenage boys and grown men, will beg, steal and borrow to own the latest pair of Jordans, Polo Shirt or Steve Harvey suit. In the meantime, hard-earned money and the potential interest from savings are lost forever. And, the purveyors of these goods (some of whom couldn't stand for you to shake their hands if asked) are smiling all the way to the bank.

In a similar manner, the financially challenged are feverishly and obsessively acquiring what is past off as precious and semi-precious jewelry. Everything from rings for the finger and ears, to chains for the neck and wrist are being sold and bought on every street corner, mall or department store without any serious regard to value.

Chapter 12 - The Crib and the Gangsta Lean - Cars and Homes

Imagine with me if you will, you are standing at a bus stop waiting for the daily 5:00 pm blue line to pick you up for your usual ride home. As you patiently wait, up drives the car of your dreams. The car that you have posted on your bedroom wall, placed as the wall paper on your lap top or the background of your cell phone. Your "Love Jones" for this car is so bad that you know every possible option and color that is available and make frequent searches on the internet to see how many are for sale in the area. Each time you see this car, your heart gets this feeling of emptiness and your mind cannot help but believe you are missing out on something because you don't own one of them. As you stare at the slowly passing car, you take a glance at the driver and passengers.

What thoughts about the driver run through your mind? Perhaps you are fighting back the feelings of envy and jealousy. Or, maybe you subconsciously confer some unfounded higher level of class, social status, glamour or attractiveness to this unsuspecting motorist.

You may not fully understand where these feelings and thoughts have their origin. Let me help you figure it out. Perhaps, it has its roots in the fact that you grew up in a time when your family could barely afford to keep a roof over your head. During these same times, you or your family was only able to afford used, barely drivable vehicles. These vehicles needed constant repair and were the focus of jokes and putdowns from even your closest friends. If things were not bad enough, every time you turned on the TV or went to the movies you were reminded what the real people in America are or should be driving. Every movie star, singer, or commercial family were driving the car you should be able to own but can not. Moreover, the sexiest and most popular songs often referred to the hottest car brands and styles. Finally, the cars you wanted but could not have, seemed to always be driven by your best friends' family or even your number one nemesis!

These feelings of inferiority and pinned up covetousness have haunted your self-esteem for years. Now, these exaggerated feelings are getting out of control. Your sub-conscious mind is working against any amount of logic and discipline you can manufacture. As a result, when the opportunity presents itself you will stop at nothing to make this long deferred dream a reality. Please note that these sub-conscious subversions of logic are in no way limited to obsessions with cars. They show up every where and in places you may not even realize. Consider how many relationships are ruined because one partner has an unfulfilled fantasy. Think about the innumerable people who believe the latest outfit will make them whole. Call to mind the status seekers who believe self-worth can be measured in carats, square feet, golf club memberships, bra cup sizes, office floor levels, eye color, inches of hair or feet from the beach.

For convenience, let us call this consuming passion, "Desert Fever". The seemingly millions who become victims to this almost incurable disease can only find momentary relief when the object of the desire is obtained. Hence, like a junkie eyeing his next "fix", the diseased will stop at nothing until this wanted relief is acquired and consumed. In the case of purchasing that long sought after vehicle, no payment term is too long and no interest rate is too high to discourage the diseased from making the deal. In many cases, the age, condition or mileage of the vehicle doesn't matter.

I distinctly remember the first time "desert fever" hit my residence. We found ourselves test driving vehicles that were well over five years old with north of sixty thousand miles. But, no one could tell us that we were not getting a good deal and this belief was only re-enforced by the envious stares and comments during our short 20 minute test drive. We could only be thankful that we thought better of purchasing the vehicle when our credit union wouldn't provide the length of contract that would have made it a viable deal.

I wish I could say that we learned our lesson and never was smitten with that disease again. However, the truth is that desert fever is never really cured only sent into remission. Only a few years later when our financial immune system was low and the economic climate was right did the dreaded illness resurface with a vengeance. During the peak of the SUV craze, we had our eye on the mid-size Lexus model. The object of our desire was a pearl white version and apparently the model year was not important. The model year did not matter partly because Lexus had just changed the body style a few years back and we knew that it would not change again for several more years. Also, we had to be flexible on the year to keep the price down. Initially, I firmly resisted the temptation and urge brought on by the fever. My remedy was based in logic and fiscal responsibility.

When we discovered that it would be nearly impossible to find the vehicle in our price range, I suggested that we purchase a SUV that "looked" like a luxury model. Talking about a case of winning the battle but losing the war! We purchased the vehicle and within less than a year I was convinced that this was one of my biggest financial mistakes. That is saying a lot, because I have made several big ones in my lifetime. No, it was not the mechanical quality of the vehicle that now caused heartburn. It was a feverish rash of resentment and discontent. Evidently, this vehicle did not provide the level of prestige and self-worth that was desired. It also provoked snobby-nosed comments from other 'pretenders' who were among our circle of friends. Now, what I described as a financially responsible decision was threatening to disrupt the emotional stability of my household. Suddenly, all of my efforts to provide a good life for my family was overshadowed by a vehicle that some of us apparently never wanted and was forced to accept and drive.

There was only one possible solution to the problem, find a way to get out of this vehicle no matter the cost! Regardless of what anybody tells you, peace is the most precious and expensive possession on earth. When you have it you will do almost anything to keep it and when you don't you would sell everything short of your soul to get it back. So, with the passion of someone trying to right the deepest wrong, I spent the next nine months looking and waiting for the opportunity to purchase that Lexus. It was my fortune (or misfortune depending on the side of the equation you stand on) to find exactly what we were looking for at a dealership not too far away. If at anytime I needed my internet searching skills to fail me that was the time. Until that web page appeared, I could say with good conscience week after week that I was doing everything I could to "solve" the problem.

It would be easiest to say we purchased the vehicle while trading in the unwanted one and everything was right with the world. But, the story hardly ends there. Like so many people, we paid way too much for the vehicle while getting way too little for our trade. With little hesitation we followed the herd, lemmings, foolish at heart, dreamers, high rollers, big ballers, and of course that infamous Jones family. As a result, we managed to double our monthly payment, significantly increase our insurance and acquire the local luxury tax rate applied to vehicles by the city and state government. The insane thing about it is that the decision became irrationally justifiable by the applause and looks of awe that were now offered by those who disdained our previous auto purchase. In some of our minds everything was now right with the world. Of course, that was the farthest from the truth.

Perhaps you are thinking that you have never experienced feelings like these. In fact you have always been able to get the car you have wanted and would more likely be that unsuspecting motorist instead of that envious bus rider. If that is indeed the case, let's think about what is going on in the head of that motorist (which is now you)!. Not many weeks go by where someone is not complementing you on your car. You see the stares, witness the unsolicited smiles of appreciation, you absorb the conferred respect and you benefit from the attention provided by the opposite sex. Now, you can't imagine existing without a car like this and it becomes as integral a component of who you are as is your last name. You also find yourself admitting that once you go luxury you can never go back.

When I received my MBA, there were many factors that led me to believe I should finally splurge and get a vehicle I really loved to drive. I had spent the last 13 years sacrificing on behalf of my wife and two children. I had always deferred my wants and needs to ensure they never went without. Although I continue to do that until this day, I was convinced (or convinced myself) that this purchase would not affect my ability to support my family.

But leaving nothing to chance, I went thru a long process of determining what I wanted to drive. What ever vehicle I chose it had to have a combination of luxury and sport. As it happened, I became infatuated with the latest model offered by Jaguar, the S-Type 4.0. I was also fortunate to find the vehicle at the price point that made the purchase "feel like the right thing to do." I was able to buy the car at 30 percent below the market value. I vividly remember the feelings I had when I rolled that vehicle off of the lot. My son, who had always looked up to me as a role model appeared ready to place another step on the pedestal on which I was perched. He couldn't believe that this gorgeous car was now ours to drive. He didn't tell me, but I suspect that he was thinking about how impressed his friends will be and looking forward to the day in the near future that he will be behind the wheel. His reaction was only the tip of the iceberg for the seemingly outrageous reactions that people had to me and this car. It seemed that every time I stopped at a light, drivers on either side of me couldn't help but look over to see who was driving. I was often greeted with smiles, nods and stares from people that spanned the cultural spectrum. On many occasions, I was stopped in parking lots by admirers of the car or perhaps me. Comments like, "Man, I want to be like you when I grow up" became the norm.

After four years of experiencing the prestige of a pauper king, I observed some incredible things:

1. No matter how poor you are a luxury vehicle automatically gets you respect among your peers and provides a sense of personal worth and success. Even if that just means winning the attention or affection of a partner.

2. As a result, individuals will struggle and assume unmanageable levels of debt and monthly payments to possess luxury vehicles.

3. Many people will spend more time and energy cleaning their cars than they do their homes or apartments. To that end they will be ready to take up arms if someone scratches their prized possession. In contrast, they will let

their homes fall apart while the latest coat of wax is barely worn before the next coat is applied.

Chapter 13 – Desert Fever is Contagious

Of course this desert fever is not limited to vehicles. It also could be a major factor in the choices that have been made in putting a roof over our heads. Believe me when I say that it is not a crime or a sin against God to desire a nice place to stay. Everyone deserves to return home from a hard, or not so hard, day of work to a dwelling that is both safe and welcoming. Moreover, we should want to be able to physically and emotionally experience the fruits of our many years of labor. In fact, this is one of my major motivations for writing this book. However, there is a right and a wrong way to attain the desired outcome.

Also, any pursuit in this direction must be seasoned with a lot of commonsense, wisdom, and the right amount of ambition. Salt is a wonderful product for enhancing the taste of food, but too much in a lifetime can have devastating results. Likewise, the conscious consumer must avoid at all cost mixing in greed covetous and pride. Many of those who find themselves among the struggling to survive have not learned this lesson.

Too often, we strive to attain apartments and homes that have no relationship to the economic realities in which we live. Therefore, young professionals seek to prove they have made it by selecting expensive apartments that create the image they want but month after month is destroying their ability to accumulate wealth or position them to buy a home. Those who are living at or slightly above the poverty line, constantly seek to find the angle to get into a nicer apartment instead of enduring the conditions that fit into their budgets until they can afford to move. For many, their less than successful efforts results in credit destroying evictions, garnishments and mounting debt. The situation is even worse for those living below the poverty line. These individuals make conscious, but uninformed choices to forego paying their rent, which is often subsidized rent for unnecessary items like a pair of Jordan sneakers for little Johnny who can't even walk yet. But, let me not get ahead of myself because I have a whole chapter devoted to the subject of clothing.

The middle-class and affluent among minorities are not that much better. In my opinion they are much worse. The impoverished can fall back on excuses like minimal resources, under-education on financial matters and the impulses brought on due to desperation. Who can blame someone striving to find a better neighborhood to live in out of fear that Johnny may be the next victim of violence or get caught up in an illegal activity that promises a way out!

The problem with the middle income and affluent is centered almost entirely on greed, unchecked covetousness and impatience. Many have bought into the unrelenting marketing of bigger, better, and finer and wear it around their necks with pride. I recently saw a home selection show where couples were seeking to buy their first home. The couple was obviously young professionals who were in the early stages of building their family. They had one child. What struck me as odd were their requirements for a home. They were calling out luxury amenities and neighborhood appearance and house size. They were shown a 2500 square feet home with more than 3 bedrooms. Their comment, "This is way too small, it is cramped!"

These homebuyers are part of a growing trend in America. People now feel entitled to the biggest and best of everything. This is even true of homebuyers that fall into every income bracket and from every nationality that is resident in America. It has become painfully apparent that the barrage of marketing, pricing wars, creative presentation of options, and "the sky will fall if you don't buy now" slogans have taken hold and gotten the typical purchaser by the throat. I am strongly convinced that this trend would have continued for many more years if the housing bubble would not have burst when it did.

Now, people can't get the quick and easy financing to feed their housing frenzy. One can only hope that this will go down as a major lesson learned for Americans, especially the poorest among us. But, as I write this I know that the traits of Capitalism supported by the roots of democracy will soon have the full power of the American marketing machine running at full speed. In fact, I am already receiving hints that the new versions of the schemes that took down the housing market and crippled the American economy are emerging in unscrupulous companies across the country.

Chapter 14 - Blame it on the Forty – the Three Mirages of Alcohol, Sex and Drugs

Out of all the traps that have hindered the ability of minorities to thrive in America, it is the strange but damaging affiliation with alcohol, sex and drugs that have sealed the fate of millions throughout the generations. Personally, I can never forget the images of people I loved whose lives were consumed and ravaged by addictions to alcohol. The worst thing about their deaths is that these family members were lovable caring and otherwise responsible people whose lives were cut short because their bodies could not handle the amount of alcohol their brains craved day after day. I begin this chapter with this personal note so that it is perfectly clear that I sympathize with the many people who have fallen victim to these fermented poisons.

Nevertheless, we must stand up and admit that the vices of drinking, drugging and sexual promiscuity has made survival and prosperity in America a perilous road for adults and children alike. Again, this is more critical for minority groups who have so many things already weighing them down. Minorities continue to spend disproportionately more on alcohol, drugs and sexual entertainment than any other group. And, how they spend their money is not even for the "top shelf" items. For instance, marginally drinkable beverages like malt liquors and cheap wines would other wise be thrown away by respected brewers and vineyards if minorities didn't allow themselves to become a lucrative market for this junk. The branding and selling of things like malt liquors is a testament to the power of targeted marketing and gullible consumers. Only in America can you find millions of Americans spending their hard earned dollars to drink something akin to sewer water and believe they are drinking liquid gold.

Moreover, these same people have been so deceived they despise the taste of "quality" alternatives to their favorite beverages. So what we have is a symbolic and disturbing tradition that plays itself out every Friday year after year. Minorities, mostly male, receiving and immediately cashing their paychecks and heading directly for the local convenience store. Unfortunately this trip is not to purchase money orders to pay bills, nor to pick up needed milk or diapers for the baby, nor the loaf of bread to complement the dinner cooking at home. Much to our dismay, these trips often end with the purchase and consumption of what is contained in a 40 ounce bottle inside a paper bag.

When we consider the trends in drug use, the picture becomes even more depressing. The impact of crack cocaine has been well documented and the devastating impact on the minority communities can be seen with or without the help of the sun. The progress of many families has been set back for generations as they struggle to overcome the lost mothers and fathers to recreational drug use. But what has not been talked about much is the incredible price minorities are paying for the explosive use of marijuana and other "victimless" drugs. Minorities are squandering millions of dollars of economic prosperity to exercise their self-given right to smoke and consume cannabis-based products.

In addition to smoking the money, the cost includes the destruction of intellectual ability, productivity and motivation. Many of our young (and not so young) men and women are pining away at home, on the streets or in jail because they could not resist the temptation to follow the crowd and an elusive buzz. In times past, ignitable products like tobacco was used as a tool to enslave minorities and the underprivileged. Now, it has become a weapon of choice for self-imposed enslavement and destruction.

Keep in mind that habit forming drugs become generational bondage because they are often visible to impressionable witnesses like offspring, siblings, friends and relatives. One of my cousins often would share at funerals and reunions how as a kid he would idealize our older cousins. He would say that as a teenager he couldn't wait until he became old enough to drink and smoke like them.

Surprisingly, he never mentioned wanting to go to work like them or taking on more responsibility. It is the things that are portrayed as cool and fun that are setting the stage for a life full of mistakes, missed opportunities and failure. I wonder if our youth would think differently if they knew that so many of the people they idealize would suffer from life-threatening disease and ailments because of the fun and cool lifestyle they were living at the time.

Chapter 15 - Gotta have the Benjamins -The relentless pursuit of Mo' Money

To me, there is nothing more sinister than the get rich quick schemes that pervade our society. The many actors in these financial dramas that play out all across our country and world are as varied as the size of the stars in the sky. I am utterly appalled by anyone who is willing to do whatever it takes to con and manipulate money out of the vulnerable and unsuspecting. I am equally empathetic to the innocent victims of these seemingly unrelenting tricks and scenes. However, I have no sympathy for anyone who willingly and knowingly put themselves in a place to get taken, because they saw an opportunity to get rich quick. While many would call those harmed in the Madoff scam victims, I see them as willing contributors. Most if not all new that what Madoff promised and attempted to deliver was too good to believe. It was their unwillingness to walk away from unrealistic high rates of return that got them hooked and left them financially devastated. The same folk who are crying foul and looking for restitution would turn down their noses at individuals expecting to hit it big in the lottery.

Although many minorities do not have the resources to get into a Madoff type scheme, they willingly throw what they have into similar schemes like multi-level marketing, work from home scams, time-shares and cheap home improvement offers. Whether they developed the idea or just signing up to gain its benefits, the root of it all is the same, greed. The Bible tells us that "the love of money is the root of all evil." When money becomes the only motivating factor for your actions and plans, it will lead you to make decisions that have devastating results for you and everyone involved.

Through the years, I have had many friends fall victim to greed and get involved in one get rich scheme or another. Often, they would invite my wife and I to join in on the opportunity of a lifetime.

Common phrases like "Its time to get in on the ground floor and watch the money roll in" often followed the "Hey, can we come over to share with you this great new (fill in the blank) we just discovered?" We also have friends who bought into the irresistible timeshare communities that seem to be everywhere. You hear them throw out phrases like, "RCI is much better than II when it comes to perks and locations." However, after a year of payments, maintenance fees and vacations that don't live up to the hype, they either suffer in silence or come up with some reason they had to get rid of their investment. Their involvement in multi-level marketing schemes nearly always ends up the same way. What makes these schemes live on or re-emerge in a different form ready and able to take down more victims? It is not the fact that they are more clever and persuasive. It's not event that they have better track records when it comes to success. Rather, it's because those who fall into the traps, refuse to admit their mistakes or are blind to the fact that these things are doomed to fail. They will not speak up to warn others that danger is ahead or they are under some form of delusion that tells them they were only moments away from the big break.

Chapter 16 - Can you Hear Me Now?

If I presented to you the phrase 44 to 22 without any additional context, you may have a difficult time figuring out to what I was referring. You may venture to guess that I am speaking of the score at the end of the last Indianapolis Colts and Miami Dolphins game. In my world, that would mean the Dolphins had won the game. You might also think that I am referring to a phenomenal performance by one of the NBAs elite players in a game the night before. The financial savvy may postulate that I am referring to a stock split for a rising corporation. Yet others may say that I am suggesting the latest Black Friday deal on DVD players at a retail chain. However, they all would be wrong.

In the recent socio-economic data published by Neilsen they astonished me by indicating that African-Americans spend more than 44 minutes a day on average talking on a cell phone. That is compared to 22 minutes for white Americans. Hispanics were a close second in the average minutes they spend with a cell phone close to their mouth or ear. It is not a stretch to assume most of this time is not spent crafting financial deals or seeking better employment but on idle chatter. This means that the two most economically challenged groups in America spend twice as much time using a device that adds little to nothing in financial value. In fact, since the cost of cell phone ownership is highly correlated to the number of minutes used these groups are contributing a disproportionate amount to the bottom line of major carriers. If you couple this with the anecdotal hypothesis that these groups also spend way too much of their money on the latest gadget in cell phones, ring tones, smartphones and camera phones it is a bleak picture.

I am also thoroughly convinced that the trend will not change anytime soon. In fact, by all indications it will probably get exponentially worse with each passing generation. Any trip to the mall, community park, local sports event or beach will reveal to you the future for cellular usage in America. I've seen toddlers who are barely out of diapers with cellphones strapped to their belts. Our babies are speaking their first words to mom, dad or grandma on a pre-paid phone purchased through the local Wal-Mart. In a recent television news story focused on innovative ways to effectively teach our school aged children, the heads of the cutting edge schools were touting the benefits of texting to keep the children engaged in the learning process. The obvious next step is to make cellphones as commonplace as textbooks in the classroom.

Another sign of the times, is the move away from land line telephones. A few years ago, the number of cellphones in service surpassed the number of households that had active land lines in the home. Even the middle-aged demographic is arguing for the expansion of cell phone usage and finding it hard to imagine their lives without a cell phone. It is not a stretch to surmise that the landline phone will go the way of the cassette tape, VCR and other dinosaurs whose time has come and gone. In a recent conversation with a close friend, she confessed that the only reason she maintained a land line is to support her home security system.

So what is the big deal here? Why should we be concerned about this trend? What is the real danger. First, lets talk about the loss of control and the significant level of dependency that is being created. Land line phones have for many years been a proven and settled technology. The only major advances in the last 25 years have been cordless phones and cordless phones with stronger signals. This has led to very stable and relatively cheap cost of ownership. No real significant barriers to entry exists and what have been normally disqualifying factors could be easily circumvented with a little bit of wisdom and savvy. There is also no real marketing strategy that could increase demand and cause our vanity to get in the way of better judgement. No one is looking to make a lifestyle statement by purchasing the latest and greatest cordless phone. Therefore, the general public had become very content with the phone service in their homes and wasn't looking to it to provide any real or perceived social status. As a result, not many were in danger of driving themselves into financial trouble over a land line telephone. Of course, I have to say "not many" because there is always that remnant who allow their lack of discipline to get them into a financial mess with anything.

In contrast, the cell phone has single-handedly revived what could have been a dying industry. Without the proliferation of cell phones, the telephone industry would be as exciting as the solid waste and sanitation utilities. When it comes to marketing innovation, the cell phone industry is in the middle of the biggest boom of the late twentieth and twenty first centuries. With so much choice and expanding technology, the leaders in this industry have everything at their disposal to create and drive a nearly insatiable demand for these products and services. This has been birthed and nourished in a practically unregulated and uninhibited business environment. Nearly anything and everything is allowed to be done to the consumer as long as it is revealed in the nearly unreadable, undecipherable fine print of disclosures and "hear me if you can" advertising.

This "Wild West" environment has led to bait and hook tactics like long-term automatic renewable contracts, confusing bundles of services and minutes, pass through taxes and fees, 'gotcha' billing, single supplier phone compatibility, use it or lose it services, exorbitant early cancellation fees, expensive insurance programs, etc. As a result, unsophisticated consumers are now slaves to huge monthly expenses to maintain and keep cellular service. One need only see a week's worth of episodes on a "court drama" television show to see and hear the carnage. There is case after case where these seemingly dumbfounded litigants are dragged into court to account for thousands of dollars in cell phone bills that have helped ruin somebody's credit and financial situation. Not only are these people doing it to themselves but are willingly allowing family members, lovers, friends and casual acquaintances to stick it to their wallets. And the cell phone companies are laughing all of the way to the bank.

But if you are thinking that the financial death toll is limited to the poor and uneducated you are very much mistaken. The success of the "smart phone" is proof positive that the cell phone companies are equal opportunist when it comes to raiding the wallets of willing Americans. You can't miss the seemingly endless news coverage of the smart phone fanatics who wait for days to get the 1g upgrades. These "responsible citizens" can't wait to spend hundreds of dollars each year to get the latest phone that only represents a marginal improvement over the previous model. Often, the improvements are only corrections of what was wrong with the old phone. So, these 'lemmings' are paying these companies serious money for fixing what should have never been broken or missing in the first place. Now, these people would never consider paying an automobile manufacturer to repair a recall item on their vehicle. Nor would they pay the fanciest of restaurants for getting their meal wrong the first time. Yet, they stand in line for days on end to get a phone in what amounts to a come one come all phone recall!

To make matters worse, these diehard patrons either are too cheap or cannot afford to pay for the insurance on a less than robust phone. So, the first time the phone drops on a hard surface (and the chances are very great considering the awkward way the phone has to be handled) there is a whole lot of crying or effort to hold back tears. Now, these folks will argue that this is an investment and that they can readily get back a portion of their purchase price by selling the old phone. But, the investment argument falls apart very quickly if you just run the numbers. It goes something like this: Today buy a phone for $400 and one year later sell it for $200 to buy the next model at $500. That's spending $700 to own a phone with a minor upgrade for less than two years.

Chapter 17 - Natural Born Criminals? – Raising Generations of young men destined for jail cells

Recently, I was observing a young lady interacting with her adorable baby boy. The child had recently started walking and was just over one years old. In fact, the event I am referring to occurred during his first birthday party. After giving him his present I wanted to give the little guy a hug and a kiss on the forehead just to let him know how much I cared. My wishes were immediately dashed because the mother "wasn't feelin'" that type of affection toward her son. Her words were, " Boy, you got to be a thug to make it in the world, be tough, a thug don't give kisses!" Needless to say, I was both disappointed and outraged. I was disappointed because I know this little one needs to have the people in his life show him the tender side of emotions so that he will be able to express them. I was outraged because I believed she knew better and I recognized that she is not the only young African-American mother with the same attitude.

Scenes like the one mentioned above has or is occurring all over this country. Many of the women (and the men that fathered their children) have taken one of two stances. Some of them are intentionally training their children to be thugs and "menaces to society" while others are letting these children raise themselves. In either case the expected results are the same. These children are destined to be teenagers or young men who permanently reside in correctional institutions or have recurring reservations in a cell of the government's choosing.

As a result, we have thousands of potential productive citizens producing absolutely nothing (except mayhem) on behalf of their families and communities. These manifest as high drop-out rates, rampant wealth destroying crimes, more non-fathered children and (for the few who become productive) low wage jobs. Economic equality will never be achieved, if the human capital resident in these young men is constantly wasted. This mindset is in no way different than the actions of warring African tribes during the height of the slave trade. These tribes inflicted unthinkable destruction on each other and the African race by capturing and selling their own into slavery. When people choose to promote or fail to prevent unproductive or destructive lifestyles they are for all intents and purposes selling their posterity into bondage.

Chapter 18 - Hidden in Plain Site – Despising the Power of Education

I have several friends and family members who have worked in the public and private school systems in various capacities and in different parts of the country. Most of my personal conversations with them will inevitably lead to some mention of the current state of schools and the children they are intended to serve. I am constantly bombarded with tales of how unprepared the students are for the learning experience. I am also inundated with horror stories about the parents who do not have a clue on what it takes to support a child in education achievement.

Unfortunately, nearly all of these stories involve parents or children from minority groups. Using their words, they describe these children as undisciplined, disruptive, unprepared, rude and hopeless. But, the bulk of their disdainful remarks are left for the parents of these public school misfits. They insist that the situation wouldn't be nearly as bad if the parents or guardians were at least trying to help. The parents appear to be as big a part of the problem as the children. Many of these parents expect the schools to do the parenting for them. They also provide no assistance with homework completion, regular attendance or the administering of discipline when it is needed. How can they expect students to learn when they know they can get away with doing as little as possible and acting out without any chance of being disciplined at home?

Many of my teaching friends say that one trip to the homes of the children explains much of the problems they deal with in school. These children live in conditions that you wouldn't wish on your worst enemy. Abject poverty, young immature parents and instability is a toxic mix that will poison the potential of anyone. This is especially true if that poison has been concentrated and consumed over many generations. The dilemma that our teachers face is daunting with no clear solutions.

Of course, this has not stopped our federal, state and local governments as well as public and private school educators from pulling out all of the stops and throwing money and resources at the problem. New academic standards, more testing, charter school options, better teacher training and even fining parents for the actions of their children have either been proposed or attempted. The most ridiculous has been fining kids for drooping pants. Most of these ideas and plans have resulted in varying degrees of success none of which have made a significant dent in the problem. None of them will solve the problem until they seriously attempt to deal with the root cause, the parents and the homes.

To be fair, social services agencies and private agencies have valiantly joined the fight in an attempt to rehabilitate these parents and stabilize these homes. Some of them are actually partnering with the schools to address the parenting deficiencies and redirect the behaviors affecting student performance. However, these efforts must be on a larger, more coordinated scale in order to be broadly effective. Also, parents, grandparents, friends and neighbors must take a more radically active role in bringing the parents and children to a place where education is once again viewed as a precious commodity.

Chapter 19- If you do not believe me read the words of Others...

"America is false to the past, false to the present, and solemnly binds herself to be false to the future." Frederick Douglass, 1852

"The American Dilemma" ... is the ever-changing conflict between, on the one hand, the valuations preserved on the general plane which we shall call the "American Creed," where the American thinks, talks, and acts under the influence of high national and Christian precepts, and, on the other hand, the valuations on specific planes of individual and group living, where personal and local interests ... and all sorts of miscellaneous wants, impulses, and habits dominate his outlook." Gunner Myrdal, 1942

"Thanks to the sixties, we have a new climate of race relations in the country. Black mayors in our largest cities. Corporate executives. On the other hand, we have Depression levels of unemployment, the collapse of the public schools system, and the epidemic of hard drugs. Everything appears to have changed, yet nothing has changed. Black people are still at the bottom." Lerone Bennett, Jr., 1992

"To those Arkansans who ask how long the state will have to deal with the legacy of Little Rock: Until justice is the same for every human being, whether he or she is black or white, we will deal with it. Until the same rules apply to get a bank loan for every person regardless of who he or she is, we will deal with it.." Governor Mike Huckabee 1997

"There are so many things better for black Americans than ever before, with the promise of more, but these signs are counterbalanced by the signs of no progress in some quarters and even backward motion in others." Anthony Walton, 1993

"Most white people seem to think we've come further than most black people think we have. The twin goals of achieving racial equality and the elimination of racial prejudice continue to recede before all the advances that we have made." William F. Winter, 1997

"I almost weep when I see what has happened to the civil rights movement, the bloody struggles for racial justice …. So much that was won over the bites of police dogs, the truncheons of bigited cops, have been diluted – or lost." Carl T Rowan, 1991

"Now we hear voices in America arguing that Dr. King's struggle is over – that we've reached the promised land. Maybe they're just carried away by the arrival of the Millennium, and are deluding themselves that when the calendar turns to the year 2000, human beings will have been perfected." Vice President Al Gore, 1998

"To put it bluntly, beneath the record-breaking stock markets on Wall-Street and bipartisan budget-balancing deals in the White House lurk ominous clouds of despair across the nation." Cornel West, 1997

"The pattern of racial disparities in economic and social conditions remains painfully stark. This is not the America we want; the most unrepentant apologist for the status quo cannot dress it up to make an appealing portrait of American justice." Christopher Edley, Jr. 1996

"The present emphasis on studying the poor and the blacks implies that these are the 'problem' groups. The real problem resides in the haves rather than the have nots. What stands in the way of social advance is resistance to change on the part of the rich and powerful, their reluctance to give up even a tiny fraction of their privileges." Alexander Thomas, M.D., 1972

"Immigrants from Africa, Asia and the Pacific, Central and Latin America and the Caribbean, have made the "minority" population increasingly diverse…. The politics of divide and rule set one group against another, and encourage them to fight for the ever smaller pieces of the American pie reserved for people who are neither white, nor well off." Project HIP-HOP, 1997

"Where we had been two Americas, whites and blacks, we were soon to become three, the whites, the blacks who would now rise, and finally the millions of bottom-mired blacks who could not." Randall Robinson, 1998

"The challenge remains to harness the power of prosperity and turn it to overcoming poverty and despair.... To continue to ignore the less fortunate among us will place the nation in peril." Kelvin Shawn Sealey, 1997

"The problem of the great majority of the Afro-American poor is the problem of income inequality. In a land of extraordinary abundance, the top fifth greedily takes so much that the bottom fifth, even working two jobs, sinks deeper and deeper into poverty." Orlando Patterson, 1997

"My conservative friends seem to have a Marxist worldview that the economy is a fixed pie, that in order for the poor to get more, the rich must get less. But ... the more people included in the economy, the more growth and the larger one's slice becomes. In an economy that is producing equitable growth wealthier citizens find they may have smaller percentage of a much larger pie, but the result is greater wealth all around.

Federal programs that would alleviate conditions for the most needy in our society ... were labeled "creeping socialism." The federal government should not interfere with the free enterprise system, it was said. Yet we noted that leaders of the free enterprise system did not hesitate to turn to the federal government when they needed help. 'Socialism' was just fine when it was socialism for the rich" Andrew Young, 1996

"In the final analysis, the rich must not ignore the poor because both rich and poor are tied together. They entered the same mysterious gateway of human birth, into the same adventure of mortal life.

The agony of the poor impoverishes the rich; the betterment of the poor enriches the rich. We are inevitably our brother's keeper because we are our brother's brother. Whatever affects one directly affects all indirectly. There is nothing new about poverty. What is new, however, is that we now have the resources to get rid of it.

A nation that continues year after year to spend more money on military defense than on programs of social uplift is approaching spiritual death" Martin Luther King, Jr., 1967

The daily life of the Negro is still lived in the basement of the Great Society. He is still at the bottom despite the few who have penetrated to slightly higher levels. Even where the door has been forced partially open, mobility for the negro is still sharply restricted. There is often no bottom at which to start and when there is, there is almost always no room at the top.

All too many of those who live in affluent America ignore those who exist in poor America; in doing so, the affluent Americans will eventually have to face themselves with the question: How responsible am I for the well-being of my fellows? To ignore evil is to be accomplice to it.

The contemporary tendency in our society is to have our distribution on scarcity, which has vanished, and to compress our abundance into the overfed mouths of the middle and upper classes until they gag with superfluity. If democracy is to have breadth of meaning, it is necessary to adjust this inequity.

There is nothing but lack of social vision to prevent us from paying an adequate wage to every American citizen... There is nothing except shortsightedness to prevent us from guaranteeing an annual minimum – and livable – income for every American family."
Martin Luther King, Jr., 1967

" I refuse to let my personal success, as part of a fraction of one percent of the Negro people, explain away the injustices to fourteen million of my people … I fight for the right of the Negro people …

to have decent homes, decent jobs, and the dignity that belongs to every human being." Paul Robeson, 1949

"The Socialist says what's mine is yours. The Communist says what's yours is mine. The Capitalist says what's yours will be mine!" Timothy E Davidson, Sr, 2010

"An increasing number of white Americans will assent to the proposition that Negroes should share more fully, even equally, in the good things of American life. At the same time an increasing number are demonstrating that they are unwilling to give up any part of their share of these good things." Lewis M Killian, 1968

"America will not have racial equality until opportunities are equalized, beginning at the preschool level, to build up the supply of qualified applicants for the new jobs emerging in the information-age America. The American ideal of equal opportunity still produces rewards, when it is given a real try. It needs to be tried more often." Clarence Page, 1996

"These people who now call for the end of policies to promote equal opportunity say there's been so much progress that no more such efforts are justified. But they fail to recognize that the tap root of racism is almost 400 years long." Vice President Al Gore, 1998

"In the long run, there has to be something like equal opportunity for all kids to get a good education in this country. Better-off people will always have an advantage, but equal opportunity should be a goal, an aspiration." Albert Carnesale, 1997

"What black Americans want is no more nor less than what white Americans want: a fair chance for steady employment at decent pay. But this opportunity has been one that the nation's economy continues to withhold. To be black in America is to know that you remain last in line …[and] have much less choice among jobs than workers who are white." Andrew Hacker, 1992

"Blacks were held back for two centuries of slavery plus another century of legally sanctioned subjugation and humiliation. One does not, as President Lyndon Johnson once said, hold some people back that long, then tell them they are free to run the race the same as everyone else." Clarence Page, 1996

"Given the fact that the average white household's net worth is ten times that of a black family's and that the overwhelming majority of leaders in business, government, banking, and the media are upper-class white males, the argument that whites suffer "reverse discrimination" is absurd" Justice demands affirmative action based on race and gender to address continuing patterns of inequality in America." Manning Marable, 1997

"This whole business of affirmative actions was no problem at all till the jobs run out. It's no big thing when you're on the job. If the lion and the deer [are] both full, nobody attacks. It's only when the lion gets hungry, he really fights for the thing." Frank Lumpkin, 1992

" What needs to be stressed is that despite all the controversies surrounding affirmative action, fewer blacks now have steady jobs of any kind and their unemployment rates have being growing progressively worse relative to those recorded for whites." Andrew Hacker, 1992

Section 2: Survival Strategies

Chapter 20 - The Case for "Unconventional" Strategies

What would cause a state like Nevada to make a conscious decision to legalize prostitution? How is it that nearly every state in the Union has decided that the Lottery is a good source of revenue? How is it that young boys choose to follow in the footsteps of convicted felons and go into the life of selling drugs? How does a beautiful and intelligent young college student at Harvard or Yale choose to become a "high-priced" call girl? Why did the state of California determine that there was a good chance that its citizens would legalize marijuana? These types of logic defying questions have most people either scratching their heads or declaring that they must be morally bankrupt and are definitely driving this country away from GOD. And, these people have the right to their opinion. However, a closer look at the situation may lead others to a different conclusion.

First, let's look at what all of these groups have in common. They all, in one form or another, are facing a crisis for which traditional solutions are or have been deemed insufficient in resolving their problem. These groups have decided to pursue an "unconventional" solution to their perceived problems. California is so deep in debt it must accept the fact that they have to do something drastic and "unconventional" in hopes of getting their financial house in order. They know that they can't cut everything and layoff everyone to balance their budget. They also understand that the "well has run dry" when it comes to borrowing their way out of trouble. The billions of dollars in tax revenue from marijuana will take a big chunk out of that elephant sitting before them. Likewise, Nevada recognized this fact many years ago when they legalized prostitution.

This same logic also drives the "success" of the lottery. The public officials who pass and sustain the lottery legislation would not be caught dead playing any of these games. However, they know that the money generated is a lifeline their states cannot afford to sever.

Young beautiful and intelligent college women face similar challenges when they must figure out how to pay for the expensive Ivy League education they believe is necessary for success. The unconventional path that some choose is reached with the same rationale. They ask: How can I get enough money, quickly enough without jeopardizing my grades and walking across the stage at graduation with tons of debt? Right or wrong, they have done the math and gauged the personal consequences and decided on the "unconventional" path. The young boy born into tough surroundings cannot perpetually "dispel disbelief" and ignore the facts shaping his future. What are his real odds of success? What do the numbers say? How far did his brothers, father, friends and cousins get in pursuing their dreams? Can abject poverty really be replaced with overwhelming success like the images he sees on television? He too completes the calculus of his life and begins to make hard choices and he must make them soon in order to get "his share" among so many rivals.

The decision to take the "unconventional" approach is actually indicative of a very significant but often ignored problem in America and most industrialized countries. In America, the naïve position that dominants our thinking, values and public policy is that everyone can succeed using the most prominent strategies offered by our society. How often have you heard, "If you work hard and study, you can make it in this world?" Also, things like "You can't make it in this world without a good education." Another is "You can make it if you live within your means!" These mantras that seem to survive the ravages of time are a sort of self delusion that keeps most Americans from really understanding what they have to do to succeed. The delusion is so strong because the strategies we have works for the majority of Americans. It is the proverbial eighty-twenty rule.

According to this rule, at least 80% of Americans have a reasonable chance of success using the conventional paths and strategies. It is "presumed" that the conventional strategies can work for the 20% but thy just have to take personal responsibility and work a little harder to achieve the success they want. This belief shapes how the twenty percent are reviewed and dealt with in our society. When they do not achieve success using the conventional strategies they are labeled lazy and listless underachievers. As a result, they begin to doubt themselves and believe the labels that are attributed to them. Even worse, if they achieve success in unconventional means they are treated as criminals, second class citizens or scam artists that beat the odds.

This is devastating to those who happen to fall into this group and oppressive for minorities who represent the majority of the "twenty-percent". America and much of the civilized world must come to the realization that conventional strategies do not work for everyone. Many minorities must understand that they have to seek and develop legal "non-conventional" strategies in order to have a reasonable chance at personal and generational success. If, despite your best efforts, conventional strategies have not worked for you or most people in your circle of family and friends chances are they will never work.

Therefore, you have to begin the soul-searching and brainstorming necessary to come up with strategies that will get you and your family on the path to survival and success. You may be one of those who are in the "desert land of America" without the necessary tools to survive or the support system in place to make the difference. This book is designed to help you start on that journey. It looks at all of the key factors of the conventional approach and how they have worked against you and suggests alternatives that may help you thrive in an otherwise hostile environment. I hope you are ready for the journey.

Chapter 21 -Three Score and Ten Years?

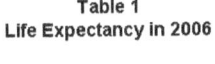

Table 1
Life Expectancy in 2006

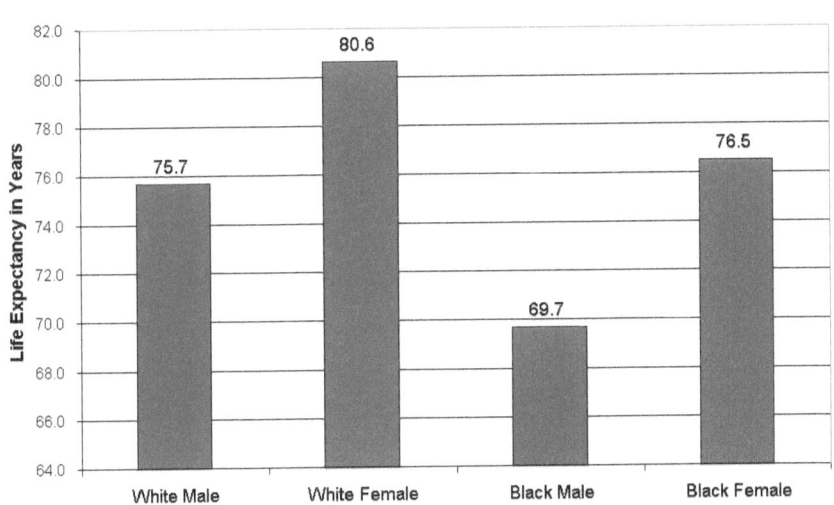

The first challenge that minorities, like African-Americans face in building generational wealth is the number of active years they can devote to wealth accumulation. Even though black women are achieving higher levels of educational and career attainment than black males, they still lag behind in income potential. Similarly, white women are making great strides in matching the income earnings of their male counterparts. Therefore, black males have as much as a decade less time to establish their nest eggs and black females face a handicap of approximately four years.

Coupled with lower and delayed growth in earnings, black households are losing hundreds of thousands in potential wealth every generation. In addition, these sobering numbers of life expectancy for blacks also means that many of them (50% of men and a significant number of women) will never collect or benefit from retirement plans and social security. If you think this is trivial, take time to consider how many retirees are able to boost their wealth by depositing thousands of dollars in social security checks each year. This is money they do not need to use for living expenses and can be (1) used to support children and grand children or (2) passed on with interest to them when they eventually pass away.

Chapter 22 - On Financial Life Support

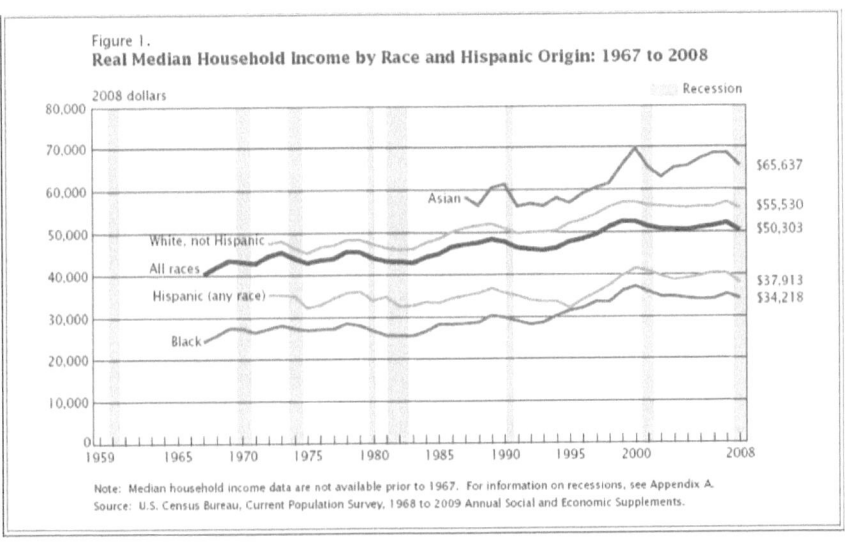

Figure 1.
Real Median Household Income by Race and Hispanic Origin: 1967 to 2008

Note: Median household income data are not available prior to 1967. For information on recessions, see Appendix A.
Source: U.S. Census Bureau, Current Population Survey, 1968 to 2009 Annual Social and Economic Supplements.

Table 2A
Median Household Income by Race 1972-2008

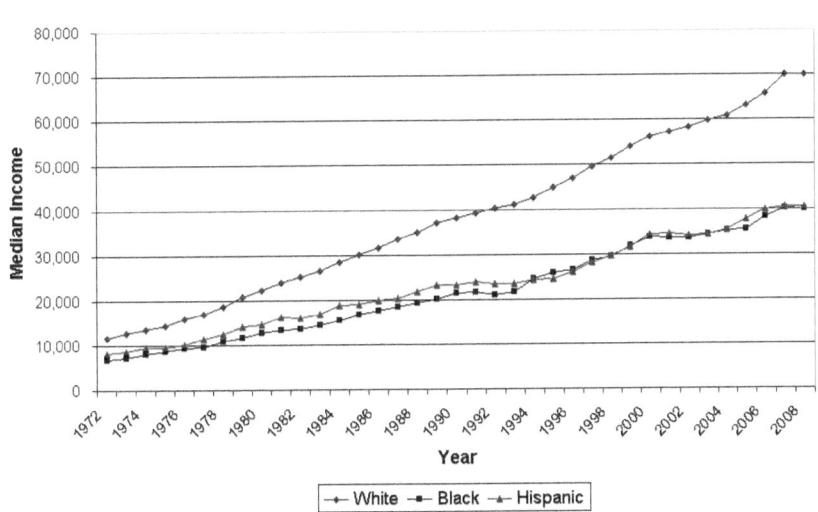

Table 2B

Table 3.
Income Distribution Measures Using Money Income and Equivalence-Adjusted Income: 2007 and 2008
(For information on confidentiality protection, sampling error, nonsampling error, and definitions, see www.census.gov/apsd/techdoc/cps/cpsmar09.pdf)

Measure	2007				2008				Percentage change (2008 less 2007)			
	Money income		Equivalence-adjusted income		Money income		Equivalence-adjusted income		Money income		Equivalence-adjusted income	
	Esti-mate	90 percent C.I.[1] (±)	Esti-mate	90 percent C.I.[1] (±)	Esti-mate	90 percent C.I.[1] (±)	Esti-mate	90 percent C.I.[1] (±)	Esti-mate	90 percent C.I.[1] (±)	Esti-mate	90 percent C.I.[1] (±)
Shares of Aggregate Income by Percentile												
Lowest quintile	3.4	0.04	3.7	0.03	3.4	0.04	3.6	0.03	–	1.27	*–2.7	1.00
Second quintile	8.7	0.10	9.6	0.07	8.6	0.09	9.4	0.07	–1.1	1.23	*–2.1	0.87
Middle quintile	14.8	0.16	15.3	0.12	14.7	0.16	15.1	0.11	–0.7	1.23	*–1.3	0.85
Fourth quintile	23.4	0.25	22.9	0.17	23.3	0.25	22.9	0.17	–0.4	1.24	–	0.85
Highest quintile	49.7	0.54	48.5	0.35	50.0	0.54	49.0	0.36	0.6	1.06	*1.0	0.84
Top 5 percent	21.2	0.48	21.1	0.31	21.5	0.49	21.4	0.31	1.4	2.63	1.4	1.70
Summary Measures												
Gini index of income inequality.	0.463	0.0045	0.445	0.0026	0.466	0.0045	0.451	0.0028	0.6	1.10	*1.3	0.72
Mean logarithmic deviation of income	0.532	0.0103	0.588	0.0075	0.541	0.0104	0.614	0.0077	1.7	2.22	*4.4	1.52
Theil.	0.391	0.0002	0.371	0.0001	0.398	0.0002	0.380	0.0001	*1.8	0.05	*2.4	0.05
Atkinson:												
e=0.25	0.095	0.0019	0.090	0.0012	0.096	0.0019	0.092	0.0012	1.1	2.18	*2.2	1.48
e=0.50	0.185	0.0030	0.178	0.0020	0.188	0.0029	0.183	0.0019	1.6	1.79	*2.8	1.28
e=0.75	0.281	0.0039	0.279	0.0027	0.285	0.0039	0.287	0.0026	1.4	1.58	*2.9	1.09

– Represents or rounds to zero.
* Statistically different from zero at the 90 percent confidence level.
[1] A 90 percent confidence interval (C.I.) is a measure of an estimate's variability. The larger the confidence interval in relation to the size of the estimate, the less reliable the estimate. For more information, see "Standard Errors and Their Use" at <www.census.gov/hhes/www/p60_236sa.pdf>.
Source: U.S. Census Bureau, Current Population Survey, 2008 and 2009 Annual Social and Economic Supplements.

Table 2C

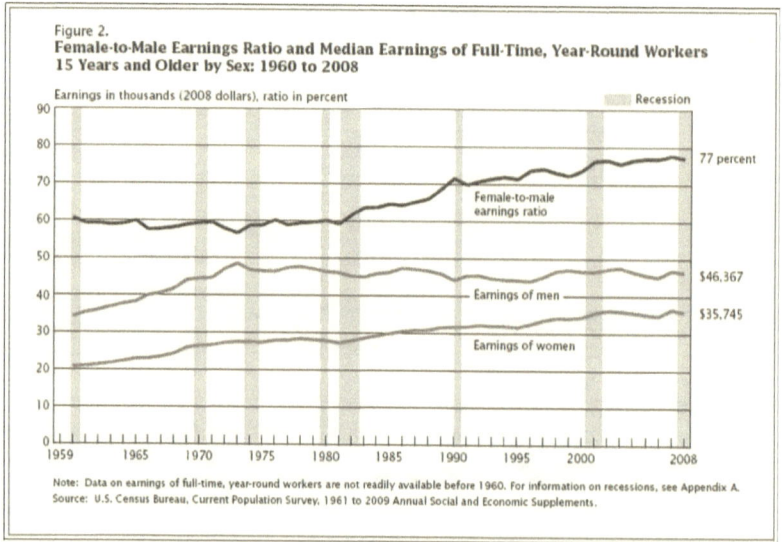

Figure 2.
Female-to-Male Earnings Ratio and Median Earnings of Full-Time, Year-Round Workers 15 Years and Older by Sex: 1960 to 2008

Earnings in thousands (2008 dollars), ratio in percent   Recession

77 percent

Female-to-male earnings ratio

$46,367

Earnings of men

$35,745

Earnings of women

Note: Data on earnings of full-time, year-round workers are not readily available before 1960. For information on recessions, see Appendix A.
Source: U.S. Census Bureau, Current Population Survey, 1961 to 2009 Annual Social and Economic Supplements.

Table 2D

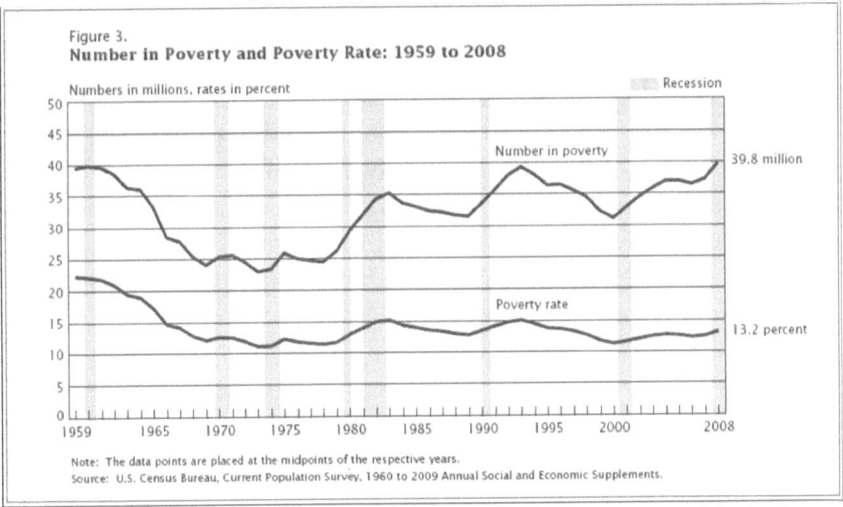

Figure 3.
Number in Poverty and Poverty Rate: 1959 to 2008

Numbers in millions, rates in percent — Recession

Number in poverty — 39.8 million

Poverty rate — 13.2 percent

Note: The data points are placed at the midpoints of the respective years.
Source: U.S. Census Bureau, Current Population Survey, 1960 to 2009 Annual Social and Economic Supplements.

For the eternal optimists who believe the cup is still half full, the numbers indicate that things are not getting any better for the poor and indigent in our country. The economic desert conditions that present themselves to the least upward mobile in our society are continuing to take its toll by sapping the "financial life" out of them. For instance, the poverty rate is increasing for children under 18 years old (19 percent in 2008 – up from 18 percent in 2007) and people 19 to 64 years old (11.7 percent in 2008 – up from 10.9 percent in 2007), while it remained unchanged for people 65 and over (9.7 percent).

It is no coincidence that the working age people are the ones who are losing ground. They have to toil in this environment trying to emerge or stay out of poverty and to build wealth. The unfortunate victims are the innocent and helpless children. Despite all of the claims to the contrary, poverty does have a lasting impact on anyone that is unfortunate enough to feel is effects. Like any other life changing experience, the longer an individual is exposed the deeper the psychological and social impact. Just as eighteen years of affluence is expected to provide a solid foundation for success, an equal number of years in poverty will certainly produce nearly insurmountable barriers to success. Anyone has the right to doubt this conclusion, but the decades of data indicating little to no progress on poverty statistics are hard to ignore.

The main point of Table 2B is to put hard data to a point that most poor people already know and rich people try so hard to de-emphasize. Based on the wealth distribution between 2007 and 2008, the poorest are still poor and the richest are getting richer. Those who represent the lowest 40% earn only 12% of the countries income. In contrast the top 40% earn over 50% of the income, with the top 5% earning a whopping 22% of the income! From the perspective of the poor, these numbers have either gotten worse or stayed the same over the last decade.

Income and Earnings Summary Measures by Selected Characteristics: 2007 and 2008 (Income in 2008 dollars. Households and people as of March of the following year. For information on confidentiality protection, sampling error, nonsampling error, and definitions, see www.census.gov/apsd/techdoc/cps/cpsmar09.pdf)					
		2008		Percentage change in real median income (2008 less 2007)	
Characteristic		Median income (dollars)			
	Number (thousands)	Estimate	90 percent Confidence interval1 (±)	Estimate	90 percent Confidence interval1 (±)
HOUSEHOLDS					
All households.	117,181	50,303	225	*−3.6	0.50
Type of Household					
Family households	78,850	62,621	423	*−3.3	0.67
Married-couple.	59,118	73,010	540	*−3.4	0.81
Female householder, no husband present	14,480	33,073	620	*−4.6	1.98
Male householder, no wife present	5,252	49,186	1,092	*−5.0	2.40
Nonfamily households	38,331	30,078	306	*−4.0	1.03
Female householder.	20,637	25,014	383	−0.8	1.79
Male householder	17,694	36,006	436	*−5.7	1.26
Race2 and Hispanic Origin of Householder					
White	95,297	52,312	250	*−3.3	0.53
White, not Hispanic.	82,884	55,530	370	*−2.6	0.78
Black	14,595	34,218	725	*−2.8	2.45
Asian	4,573	65,637	2,280	*−4.4	3.77
Hispanic (any race).	13,425	37,913	799	*−5.6	1.94

Table 2E

The most striking information presented in Table 2E is that over one out of four African-Americans are living in poverty. This rate is nearly six times as high as white Americans and significantly higher than any other minorities, including Hispanics, where one out of 5 are living below the poverty line. One other thing to point out is the subtle bundling of Hispanics with White Americans. There is a common belief among many that Hispanics are considered and treated as equals to whites in many settings. This is especially the case for non-Mexican Hispanics. This race-bias may have the impact of suppressing the number of Hispanics that fall into the ranks of the impoverished. Finally, it is interesting to note that Asians who are primarily self-employed imports have poverty rates that are equal to that of white Americans. Another potential factor influencing their poverty rate is the fact that they have not been subjected to centuries of overt discrimination.

Chapter 23 - Making Bricks without the Straw

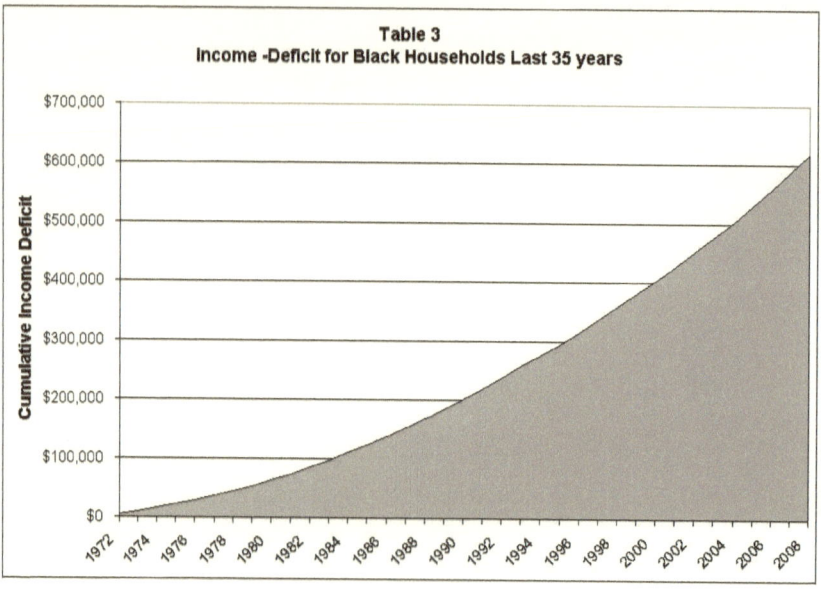

Table 3
Income -Deficit for Black Households Last 35 years

What would you and your family have been able to achieve with an additional $600,000 in earnings over the last 35 years? How much wealthier would you be if you were able to set aside and invest $20,000 dollars each year. Even with a modest rate of return of 8% you would be able to build your net worth by as much as $3.5 million. If you think this number is unbelievable, imagine multiplying that by every working adult in your immediate family. This is the crux of the argument supporting the idea of institutional economic oppression of America's minorities. One popular gospel song from the seventies and eighties summed the situation up in one title phrase; "I'm coming up the rough side of the mountain!" African-Americans and other minorities face this difficult journey generation after generation with no realistic glimpse of 'change'. In contrast, the proverbial rocks, cliffs, dangers and struggles are all too real and psychologically overwhelming. What do you do when you look up and see more mountain than your resources and strength can overcome? Do you gain strength from the slim few that made it over and believe you can beat the overwhelming odds as well? Or, do you lose heart because of the millions who have crumbled in the face of certain defeat?

Chapter 24 - Help Wanted ... But probably not You

Table 4
Comparison Unemployment Rates 2008

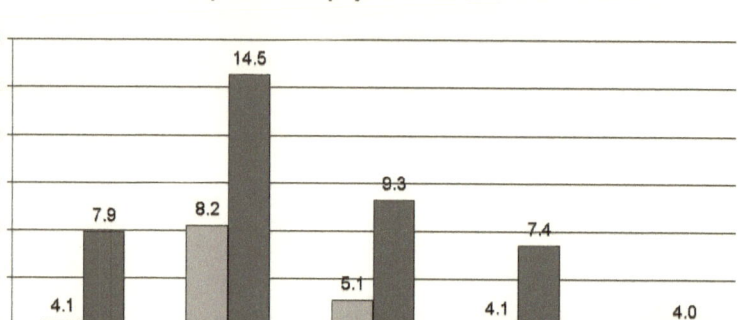

For many years there has been no debate over the fact that succeeding in the classroom increases the odds of success in employment and earnings. It would be unfruitful for me to start a debate or undermine this critical assumption about the value of an education. However, I would be remiss if I did not point out a few things that make the argument a little more complex than "graduation guarantees you will be successful in America." First, Table 4 supports the notion that high school graduation and higher levels of education makes it easier to obtain and maintain employment. Anyone who believes otherwise is suffering from self-delusion or a bad case of denial.

However, Table 4 debunks the presumption that education is the great equalizer. At every education level the unemployment rate of African-Americans is nearly twice that of their white counterparts. Unfortunately, many minorities are chasing advanced and multiple degrees under the allusion that this will improve their marketability and employment potential. However, the only real affect that this has is to increase their debt load and potentially keep the unemployment discrepancy from getting worse.

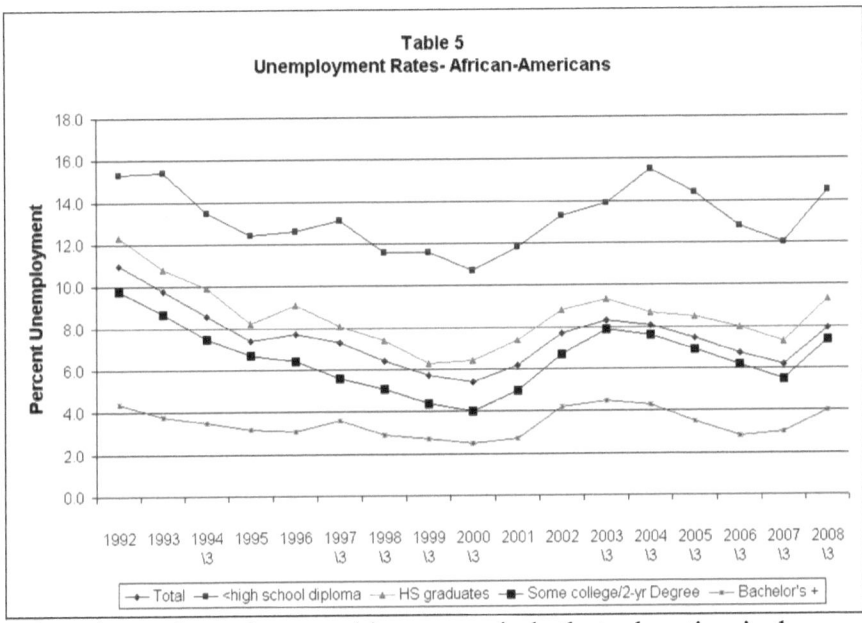

It has always been drummed into our minds that education is the ticket out of the ghetto or a mundane existence. If all else fails you can fall back on your education. Table 5 seems to support that mantra and indicates the more education you have the better your chances of gaining and maintaining employment. I can't tell you the number of people I have met who are in situations where they cannot find employment because of a lack of education. Even more alarming are the people who have lost their jobs due to layoffs and have little to no marketable skills or training to help start a new career or business. There are probably millions of people driving to work, sitting at their desk or tossing in their beds at night worried when the axe will fall and how they will support their families. They have spent years procrastinating on plans to attend school or worse yet comfortable with their current roles and under the impression that the job will always be there. This is in spite of the news reports of workers arriving to their jobs only to find the place boarded up and vacated. Some of these are dear friends or coworkers. It is literally heart-wrenching to see a coworker become a victim of an unexpected layoff or job loss when you know their prospects are slim.

Even worse are the parents who are setting their children up for failure or hardship because they are unwilling or unable to help their children obtain an education. These parents refuse to assist with college because it will put a cramp in their lifestyle. Others refuse to help or find help for children who are obviously struggling through school. Perhaps part of this mindset is due to the fact that they didn't learn the value of education when they were growing up and still view it as optional. Still others just don't see the point and have given up on these struggling children and resigned them to a certain level of achievement. For these children, the military, local shipyard or plant, mega-department store or farm is their best and only bet. Ironically, many of these parents will spend their last dime to get these children gaming systems, cell phones, designer clothes, name brand shoes and even cars! Some how they can rationalize these choices to the detriment of their children and the generations to follow.

Chapter 25 - Putting Too Many Eggs in the Education Basket

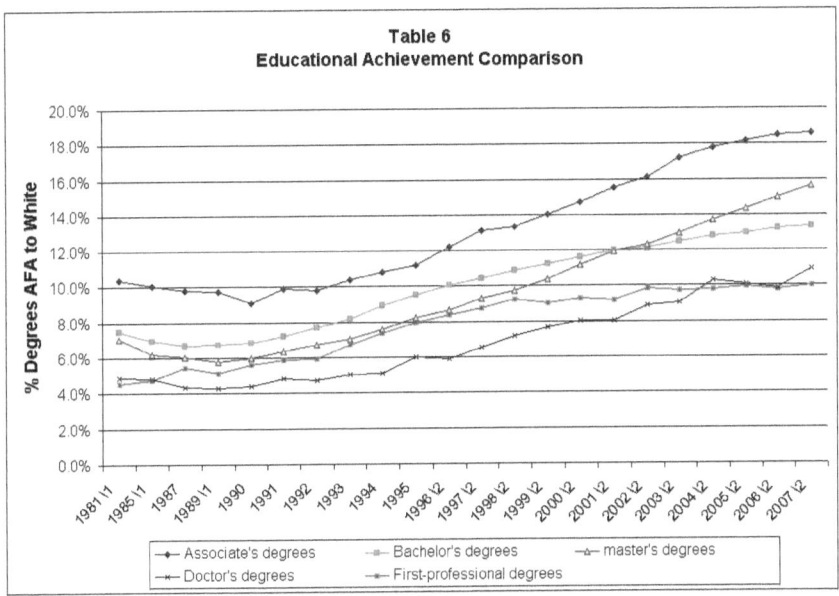

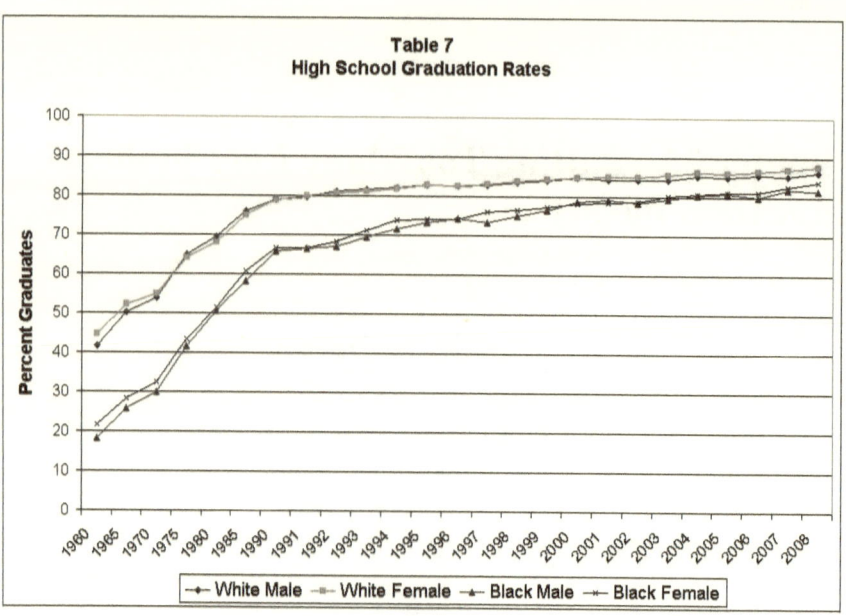

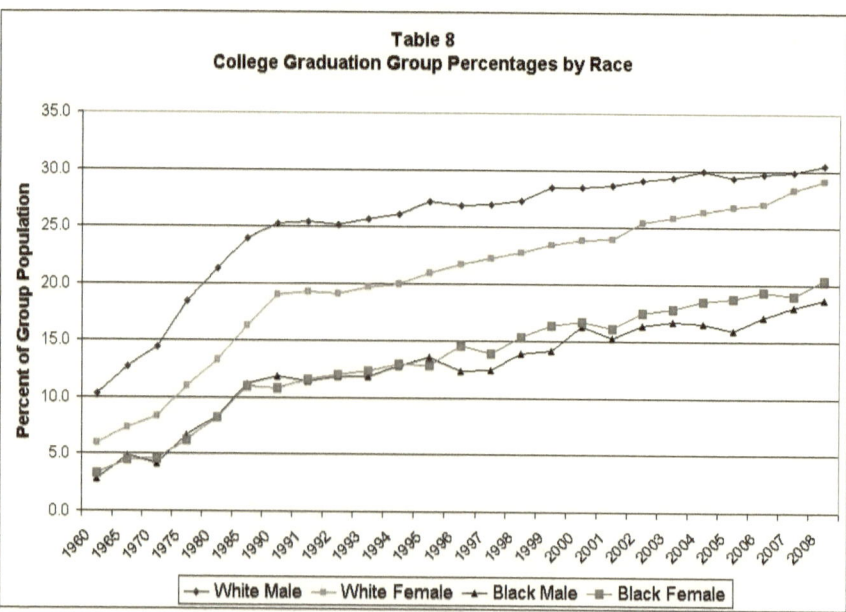

So, I just made a pretty strong argument for the value of a good education and educational attainment. It would make you think that I believe education has and is working for all of America the very same way. So, to counter that perception I have inserted Tables 6

through 8. These tables help balance the scorecard on the value of education to the typical minority.

Although these numbers reflect the status of African-Americans, it would not be a big stretch to apply this to other groups like Hispanics and especially those of Mexican decent. These charts show that at nearly every level of academic achievement, the percentage of African-Americans to White graduates have steadily increased over the last 30-50 years. In fact the differences in high school graduation rates are statistically insignificant! What affect has this had on the economic disparities faced by African-Americans?

Well, apparently when it comes to unemployment rates absolutely nothing. If you refer back to Table 5, at nearly every level the unemployment rate has remained fairly consistent. And, as you will see later on in this book, African-Americans don't fair much better when it comes to income and wealth generation. We will show that education is a vital tool, but far from a panacea for solving the economic woes of minorities. Of course, we can debate for the rest of our lives the reasons for this paradox but I choose to take the stance that things will never really change. When things don't change, relying on the same remedies is not only foolish, but self-defeating.

Chapter 26 - Fifteen Minutes can get you an Unfair Rate

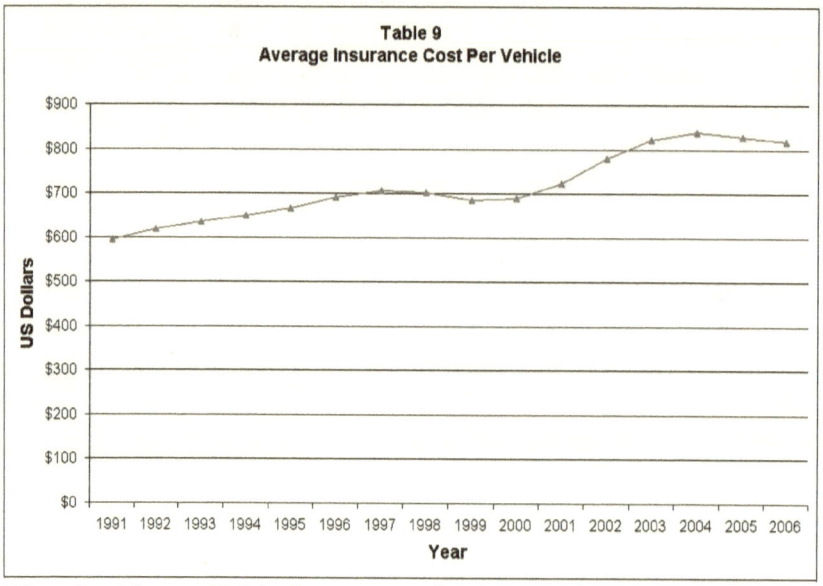

When looking at Table 9, you may be tempted to ask "What is so important about rising insurance rates? How does that impact the economics of African Americans and other Americans?" Well, the answer to these questions is twofold. First, consider the fact that auto insurance rates are heavily influenced by credit scores and payment histories. That means a driver can have a flawless driving record and still pay much more than someone else who has a better record of payments. The higher premium quotes leads those impacted by them to often choose less coverage and higher deductibles in attempt to keep it affordable.

This is a classic case of having to pay more for less. Other things to factor into the equation are the extra cost of paying the premiums over time, higher down payments and very little forgiveness for late payments or claims. In many states, a proverbial "stick" is administered by the Department of Motor Vehicles in the form of stiff uninsured motorist fines. As a result, many minorities are stuck in a yearly battle to obtain and maintain mandated insurance that only truly helps the companies that offer them. Even worse, they often are unable to benefit from the insurance because many of their policies are "liability only" or they can't afford the high deductible. Chances are at some time during the course of your travels today, you will see at least one vehicle with dents and dings that are left unfixed because of no coverage or a deductible that is too high to afford.

By the way, auto insurance is a perfect example of how the prevailing financial advice does not speak to the needs of the poor. Most if not all financial advisors would tell you to keep your deductible high in order to get a better rate. However, they are speaking to those individuals who have reserve funds that are substantial enough to cover the cost of their deductible. For this strategy to be affective you really need to have set aside at least enough to cover every car you have twice. For instance, if a couple has two vehicles and each of these vehicles has a $500 deductible, they will need to set aside $2000 to be safe. This is because they will otherwise run the risk of not having the funds to cover a second incident until they are able to save the money. For families near or slightly above the poverty line, this reserve represents nearly 10% of their annual income and funds that they would probably have to spend in order to make ends meet.

Chapter 27 - Uncle Sam wants You... Really!

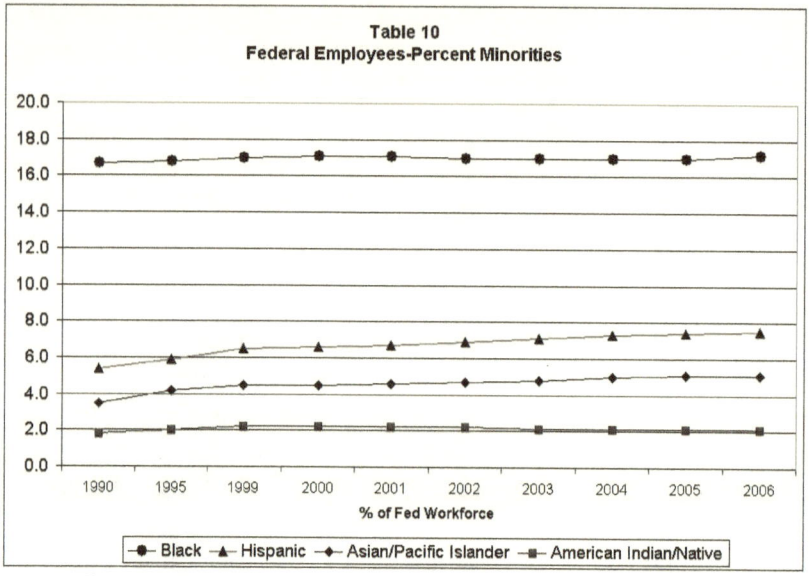

According to official statistics, African-Americans represent only 12% of the US population. When you account for the number in prison and in situations that are not typically accounted for, the percent of employable African-Americans is even less. With that in mind, the results shown in Table 10 are quite remarkable. Why is nearly 17% of the federal workforce African- American? Does this indicate that seeking and landing a job in the federal government is a more effective strategy for economic success than obtaining higher levels of education? Is the Federal government actually keeping the unemployment levels for African-Americans down by hiring so many into government jobs? Is this why so many political groups are seeking to shrink the government? And most important, am I the only one who has noticed this contradiction?

Again, I am not attempting to answer any of these questions but simply offer them as food for thought. However, I do want you to seriously reconsider your strategy for pursuing and obtaining success in this supposed land of opportunity. I want every economically disadvantaged person in this country to see the world and their personal situation through their own eyes and not the eyes of others who more often than not do not know what is best for you. I was recently reminded of that when I happened to see a seen from the classic movie "Coming to America." In this particular scene, one of the workers in the restaurant was 'encouraging' other workers about the path to success as they work their way up the ranks from washing lettuce to making fries to store manager. The obvious lesson it tries to convey with humor is the futility associated with trying to move your way up the ladder to success using somebody else's strategy.

Chapter 28 - Unable to Own a Piece of "The Rock"

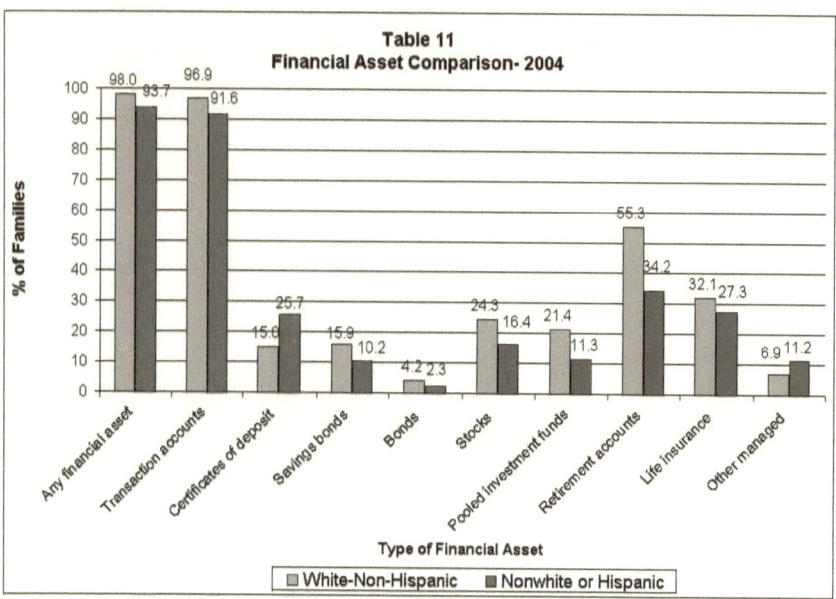

Table 11
Financial Asset Comparison- 2004

There is nothing more telling on the economic disparities that exist in America than with the possession, use and management of financial assets. It is not surprising to learn that a relative amount of parity exists when it comes to the use of transaction accounts like checking, savings and money markets. In the era of direct deposits and debit cards, it is almost inconceivable for someone to completely manage their money without at least one of these assets. But, (stating the obvious) parity in the number of accounts doesn't mean the amount of resources in those accounts are in any way equal. In fact, merely having a checking or savings account is a very poor indicator of wealth or economic well being. For that, you need to look at who holds many of the other instruments listed in Table 11.

First, it is interesting to note that minorities hold a disproportionate amount of the Certificates of Deposits. The potential reasons for this are as elusive as they are varied. It could be because these are relatively safe investments for groups who have limited funds to save or invest. Perhaps, it is because CDs are uncomplicated investments that make it easier to explain to the users and therefore, are a logical next step up the investment ladder. It is also possible that minorities for some reason mistakenly believe that CDs are their direct ticket to building wealth.

However, when it comes to the true indicators and generators of wealth, minorities lag behind by 'landslide type' numbers. The most significant of these are stocks, pooled investments and retirement accounts. This is neither by accident nor a matter of choice. This is primarily the result of existing resources, access and support. Inheritances and gifts lay a solid foundation for growth in these categories. Higher levels of income, job benefits and connections add on tiers that truly separate the 'have much' from the 'have some', and those that 'have little' of these wealth building tools.

Another vital differentiator of wealth and economic stability is life insurance. However, its effectiveness in maintaining and building wealth is highly dependent on one's ability to acquire affordable life insurance in the amounts needed to keep pace or make up for deficiency in income. We have already discussed how factors such as health, life expectancy and predatory practices make this a substantial obstacle.

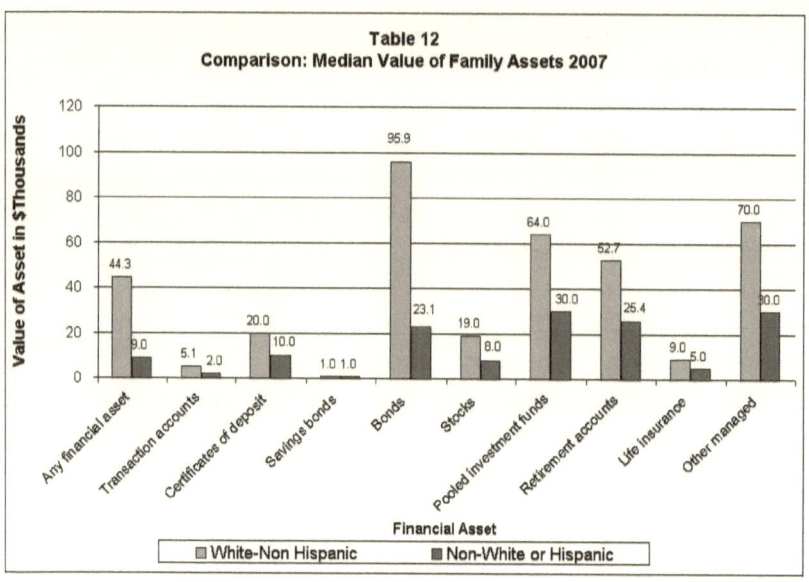

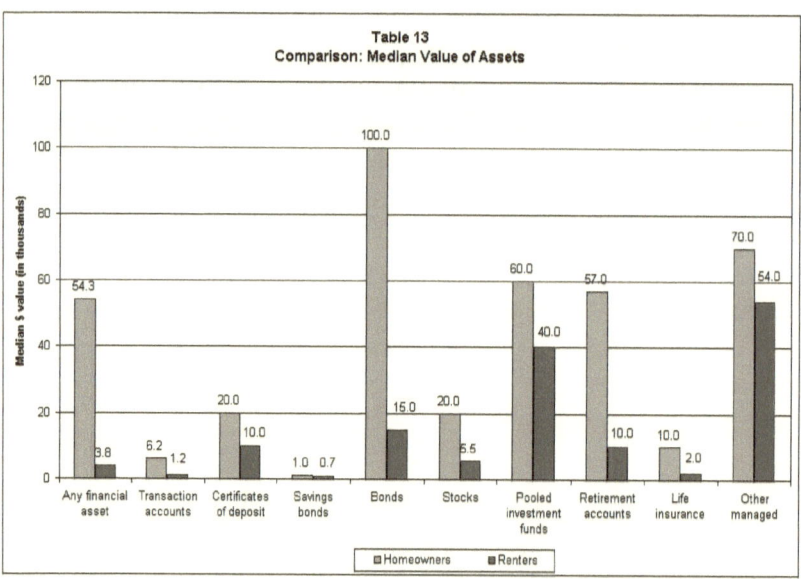

Does the mix of assets matter in how much wealth you accumulate? Or, does the amount of wealth influence and dictate the type of assets you possess? By rearranging and analyzing the information in Tables 12 and 13, we may get an insight into possible answers. Minorities typically hold the majority (80 plus percent) of their wealth in the same set of assets (bonds, 'other', pooled investment funds and retirement accounts) as mainstream Americans. However, the amount of wealth held in these assets is typically much less in every category. The average amount held in bonds is only 25% of the mainstream group. Likewise, the mainstream group holds more than twice as much in pooled investment funds and retirement accounts than the average minority. Additionally, the mainstream investor has more than twice as much as the typical minority in the mysterious 'other' asset category. In sum, the average mainstream investor holds $340K in assets as compared to $136K for the typical minority. Finally, although minorities own a disproportionate number of CDs, they are obviously held in significantly smaller quantities because the average amount held in CDs is about one-half of the mainstream group.

Some may use this data as an indication of progress or as a directional indicator of the path to financial equality. That is, all minorities have to do is keep moving in the direction of emulating the investment strategies of the mainstream group and widespread economic success will only be a matter of time. However, these individuals will have not taken into account how difficult it is to emulate the historical support that serves as the incubator for the success of those in the mainstream. Also, many of the big four investment vehicles have barriers to access such as investment floors, knowledge and awareness. How can you invest when you do not have the $5000 minimum initial deposit? How will you be able to invest in something that your job title does not make you eligible? How can you get in on a lucrative IPO if you do not have the inside information and connections to buy the shares at the optimum price? How do you obtain the services of a financial advisor who will share the same advice he offers his 'other' clients?

Chapter 29 - From American Dream to American Fantasy

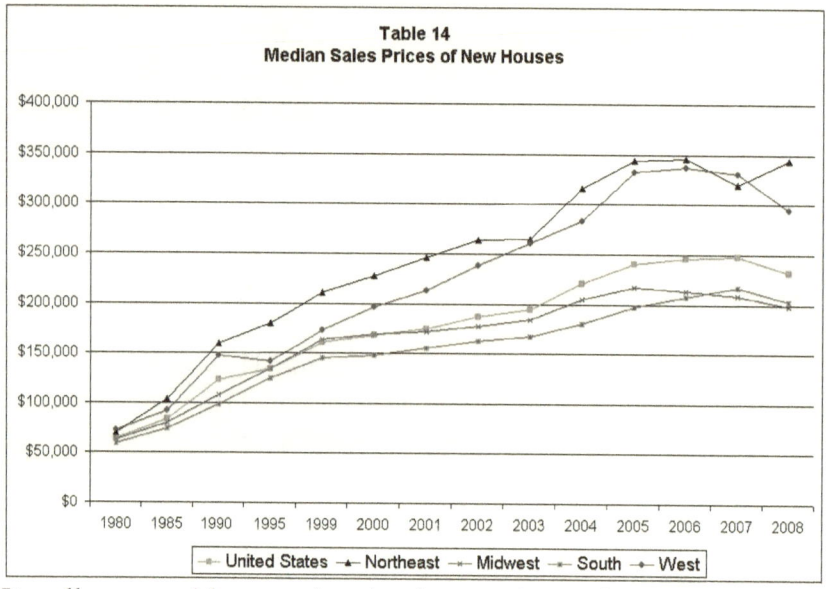

Table 14
Median Sales Prices of New Houses

Legend: United States — Northeast — Midwest — South — West

It really goes without saying that income is not the only determiner of how much financial wealth you will be able to accumulate over your lifetime. One must also consider how much you have to spend to live and thrive in America. For instance, where you live and how much you pay for that housing directly impacts your ability to save and invest. Until the housing crisis in 2008, all economists, financial advisors and housing market prognosticators were singing from the same sheet of music. The song they were singing to seekers of the American dream was a symbiotic lullaby compelling them to believe that purchasing a home was the most realistic way to financial independence. The resulting chorus seemed to be a self-fulfilling prophecy as everyone from developers to contractors to real estate agents joined ambitious homeowners in benefitting from the sky rocketing home prices. To the average and not so average American this investment was a no-brainer. We could and would continue to grow our wealth as the ever bigger and more lavish houses would increase in value and support our insatiable need for expendable equity.

The inevitable collapse of the housing market has had a definite and devastating impact on minorities that could last for decades to come. It could easily rival the crippling impacts of Reconstruction, Jim Crow, Red lining, FHA abuse and welfare reform combined. The resulting elevated home prices (don't confuse this with house values) have trapped people in homes they cannot afford and blocked them from owning homes that they would like to own. The revisions to loan requirements and the artificially conservative risk positions of lenders have set minority home seekers back at least a hundred years.

After consuming a major dose of reality, current homeowners will come to the realization that the 30 percent reduction in the value of their homes may never be recovered. Homeowners now face the new paradigm where (save for the tax exemption) the value of houses is not much different from purchasing a car. Once you figuratively drive it off the lot (i.e., are handed the keys at closing) the value of your new possession is suspect and up to interpretation. Worst yet, those who lost their homes to foreclosure, short sales and title surrenders have been hit with a penalty that will be more debilitating than a chapter 7 bankruptcy. This does require a deeper explanation.

The credit bureaus, for some unexplainable reason, have been given the power to establish credit ratings that are for all intents and purposes treated as the gospel regarding an individual's financial integrity. Although the details of their formulas are not published, their predictive models use credit history, number, amount and type of credit lines and other factors to provide a score representing the amount of risk anyone may pose to prospective lenders. These models have not been adjusted to account for the tsunami of foreclosures the first wave of which are now hitting the shores of every state in the union. Many of those affected may never be eligible or in a position to buy a home again. A large number of those caught in the crisis are left with poor credit, additional debt and no place to call their own. The ultimate reason they may never recover is the psychological and emotional damage done that obliterated the confidence needed to rise from the ashes of this disaster.

I wish the horror story they find themselves in didn't have a second act, but it does. Those fortunate enough to find a place to rent or lease must face the rising cost of renting that is a direct result of the mortgage crisis. It is a simple case of supply and demand. The high demand has been created by hundreds of thousands of previous homeowners looking for affordable places to lease. The supply of available rental properties has been stifled by the tightening of credit by banks making loans to would be developers. This short supply and higher demand has and will lead to higher rent for everyone. As the price of rent escalates to the level of mortgages (more than 30 percent of income) it will keep the renters from paying down debt and saving the now mandatory 10 to 20 percent needed for a down payment.

Mr and Mrs White were a solidly middle- class minority couple within ten to fifteen years of retirement. Although they made significant incomes, both of their jobs were highly dependent on the health of the housing industry. Eight years before the housing bubble burst, they had worked their way into a position to build their dream home. Built from the ground, this home had everything they wanted and would serve as their retirement home. They had raised all of their children and the youngest was heading for college when the crisis hit. As the housing market headed for free fall, both of their sources of income vanished quicker than anyone could imagine.

Although the White's struggled to hold on to their dream, they finally had to succumb to the inevitable. For the Whites, the death of their dream came in the form of a short sale that left them owing $30,000 and having to leave a neighborhood and friends in a way that no one expected. How does a family like the White's recapture the dream? Must they resolve themselves to the fact that their dream is over? Will they be better served by resigning the rest of their lives to living in a rental? Would it be realistic to encourage them to try again and to never give up home ownership?

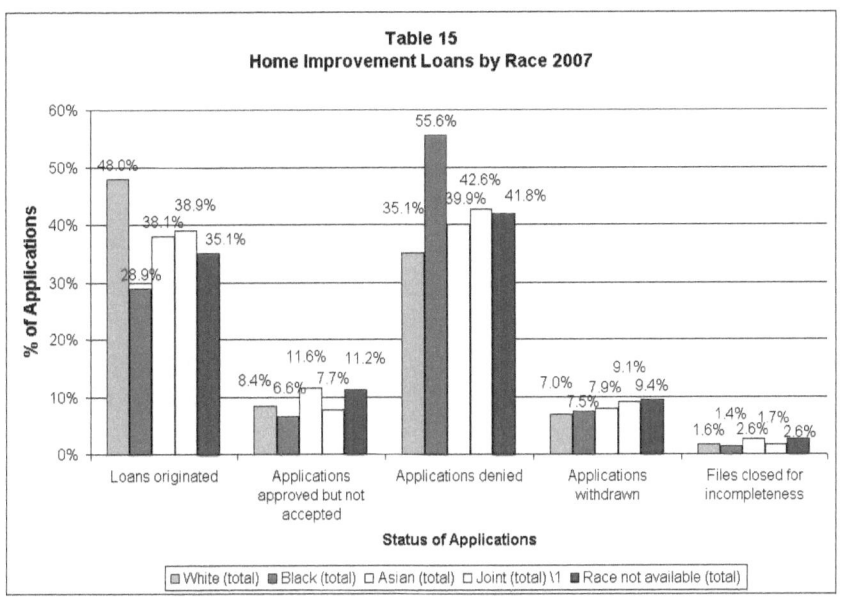

Table 15
Home Improvement Loans by Race 2007

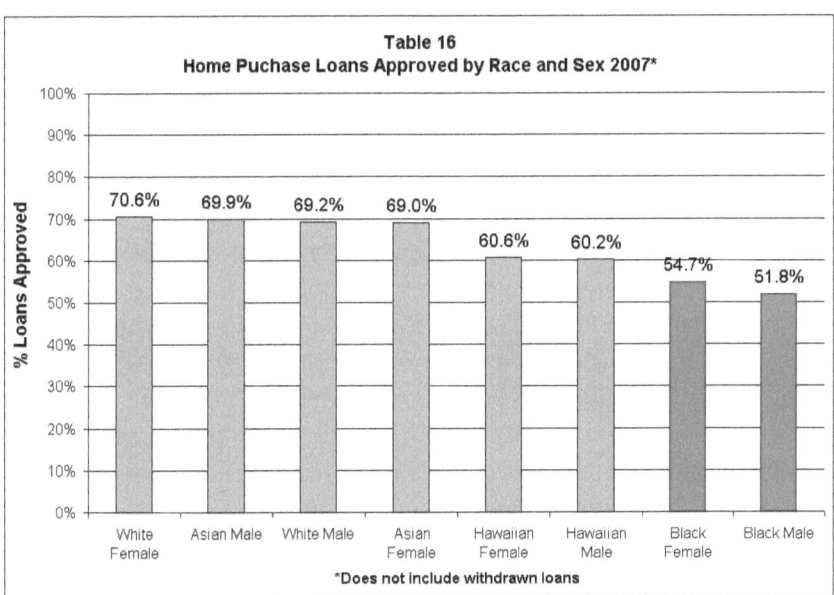

Table 16
Home Puchase Loans Approved by Race and Sex 2007*

Let's suppose for a moment that homeownership was the path to financial security for Americans. Then, the next logical step is to ask whether access to or navigation of that road is the same for all. Is it equally likely that a minority can obtain a loan to purchase or improve their home? Tables 15 and 16, should provide an answer to that question. Immediately, we notice that nearly all groups have brought into the notion that seeking to purchase a home is a good thing. A large percentage (nearly 30% and above) of these groups are at least pursuing home ownership. The lag for African-Americans could easily be attributed to a disproportionate number living in poverty where home ownership is impossible. Unfortunately, the road gets pretty bumpy for minorities once the decision to make a purchase is made. Of those applying for loans, minorities consistently have significantly higher decline rates. Who would have imagined that an African-American would have better odds of winning a coin toss than getting a mortgage loan approved? The disparity would be even greater if you factored in the number of withdrawn loan applications.

It is also important to note that race and gender play a role in approval rates. While 70% of white women can expect to be approved for loans, only 54% of black women can expect the same. And, what some may find shocking (I am not one of them), black men have the lowest approval ratings by a large margin when compared to every other group except black females.

What are the implications of these findings? Although, black women have made significant strides in education, career growth and income, they are not much more likely to get a loan approved than black men who have declined in nearly all of these categories. Asians have either been able to break the code on mortgage success or have been elevated to the same levels of risk as their white counterparts. What role does financial literacy play in these statistics? Could we argue that black women, in all of their getting, have not gotten how to manage their new found financial resources? Or, do the challenges they face to achieve financial equality go beyond stable employment and better income?

Chapter 30 - Closing the Graduation Gap: A Thin Silver Lining

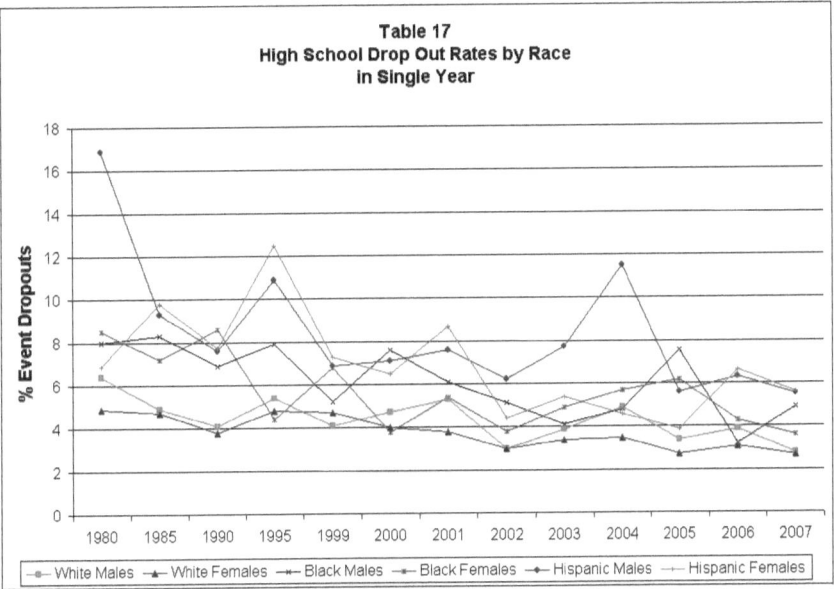

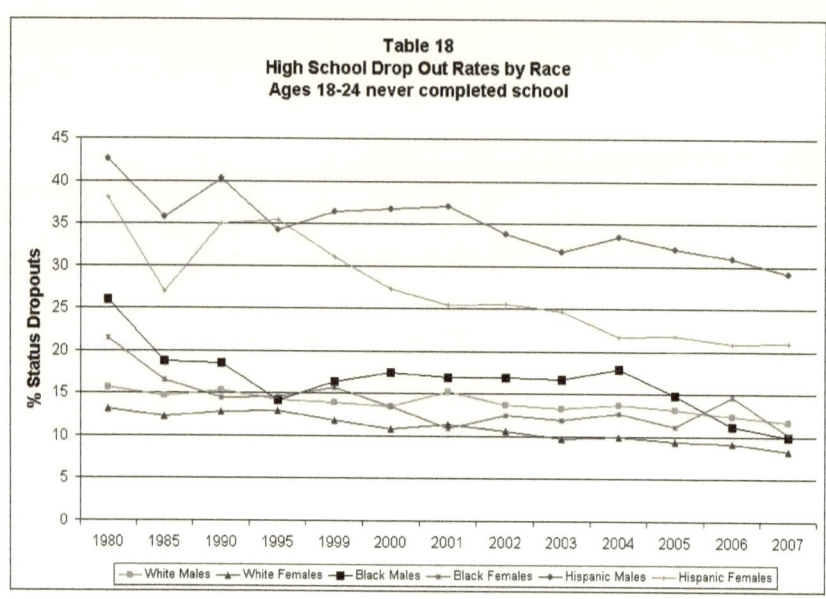

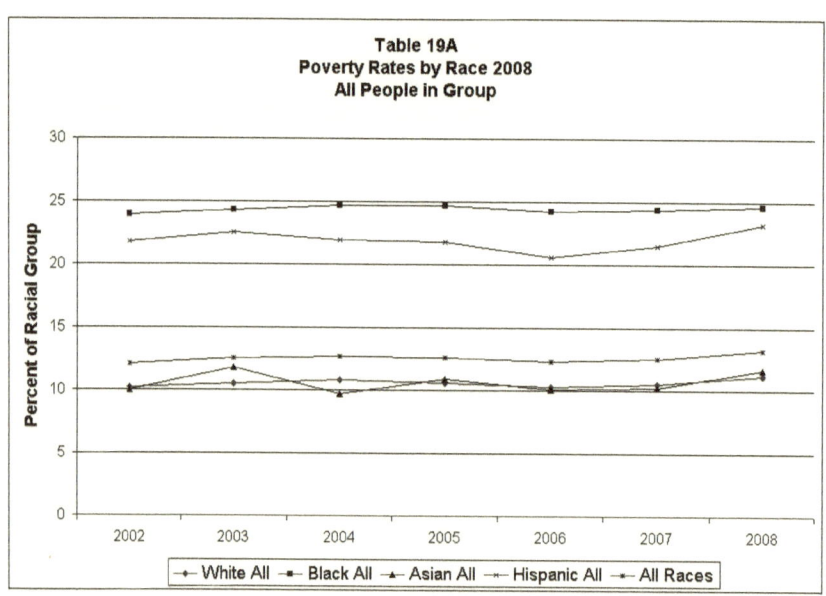

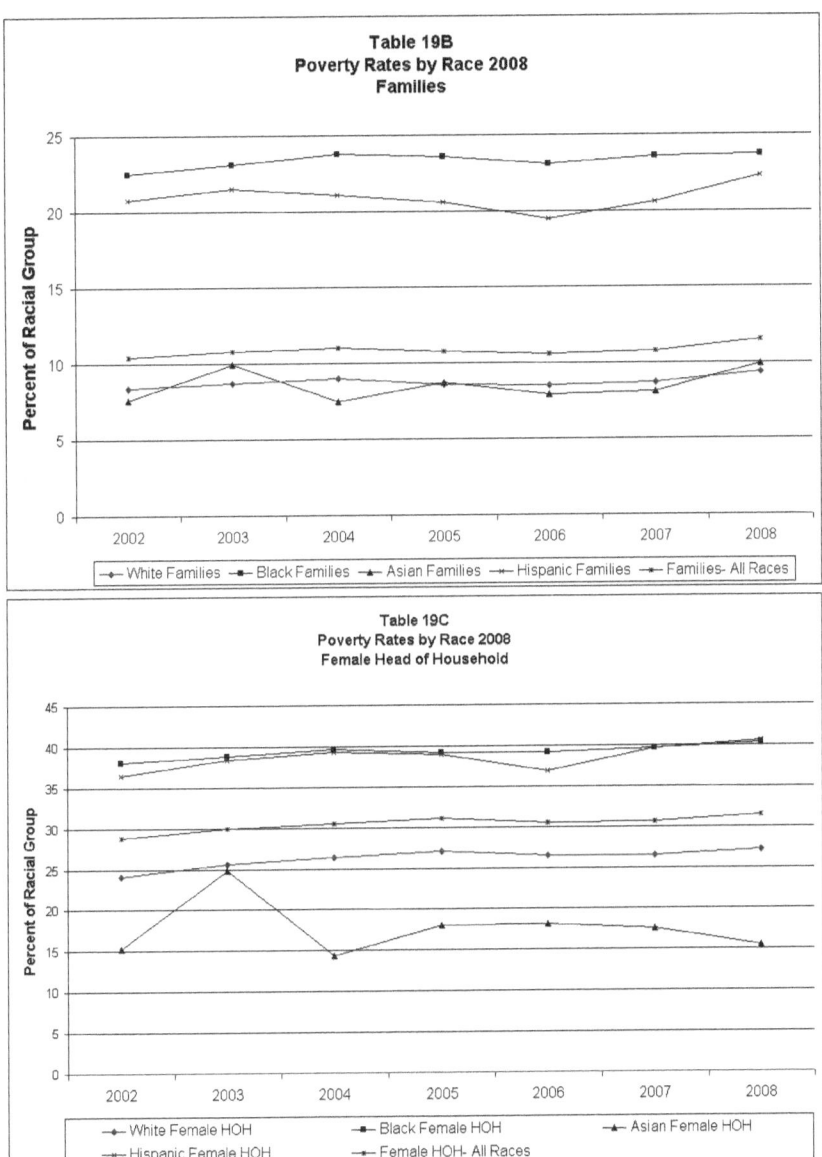

Table 19B
Poverty Rates by Race 2008
Families

Table 19C
Poverty Rates by Race 2008
Female Head of Household

Tables 17 thru 19C tell a compelling story in that they dispel one of the biggest myths. First, contrary to popular belief the dropout rates for high school students has steadily decreased for all races. And, the dropout rates for minorites have been dropping at a rate that is higher or equal to every one else. This has resulted in comparable drop rates. Unfortunately, these improvements had absolutely no impact on the proverty rates for minority men and women regardless of their gender of family status.

Chapter 31 - SAT and GMAT: Don't Believe the Hype

The Fair Test Group has been able to provide some myth busting for those who may rely on or are skeptical of standardized test: Read this excerpt from their website below:

Myth #1. The SAT gives all students an equal shot at college admission
The biggest issue is with the way the test is constructed. It rewards strategic guessing, has highly-speeded pace, and includes too many cultural biases. Therefore, the SAT denies African Americans, Latinos, Native Americans, and women equal opportunities for higher education. Research shows that when admissions offices place heavy emphasis on SAT scores - particularly when they use rigid cut-off score minimums - the number of qualified students of color and low-income students admitted goes down. What's more, using scores to award scholarships prevents students of color and women from getting their fair share of badly-needed tuition aid.

Myth #2. The SAT score gaps merely reflect differences in students' academic backgrounds
Regardless of how the data is sliced, there are still large gender and racial gaps in their SAT scores. A federal court reviewed the test-makers' best arguments, which took into account variables such as ethnicity, parental education, high school classes, and proposed college major, and concluded that "...[U]nder the most conservative studies presented in evidence, even after removing the effect of these factors, at least a 30 point combined differential [between males and females] remains unexplained."

Myth #3. SAT scores are precise
The College Board's ATP Guide long stated, "Users learn to understand and appreciate the meaning of a score of 430 in the same

way that they have learned to understand and appreciate the meaning of, say, 14 inches..." But it notes in other publications that the SAT's margin of error is approximately 60 points. Even more incredible, the test-makers admit that two students' scores must differ by about 120 points before anyone can be sure that the differences are meaningful. Adding to the confusion, ETS "re-centered" test scores in 1995. This changed the formula used to convert raw scores into the SAT's 200-800 point scale, resulting in an average score increase of nearly 100 points. If the SAT is a "common yardstick," as the test-makers say, it must be made of elastic.

Myth #4. The SAT is more accurate than high school grades

On the contrary, despite all the differences between courses and grading standards, high school grade point average (GPA) is still the best predictor of first year college grades -- which is all the SAT claims to predict. As a student moves through college, SAT scores become even less accurate predictors, with high school GPA and rigor of courses trumping the SAT in forecasting bachelor's degree attainment. This shows just how inaccurate the SAT really is.

Myth #5. Colleges still need test scores to make admissions decisions

Now, hundreds of colleges and universities admit a substantial number of applicants without regard to test scores. This shows that you can have a rigorous admissions process without the SAT. Highly selective institutions can follow the examples of other colleges that found the diversity and quality of its students improved after they made the SAT optional 25 years ago. Fewer than 150 colleges in the country reject more than half of their applicants. Admissions officers at these schools have many other ways to deal with differences in high school curriculum and quality.

Myth #6. When girls and boys are matched by ability, the score gap on the SAT-Verbal section disappears

The College Board's way of "matching by ability" is to match test-takers' SAT scores! So if the test is flawed as an overwhelming body of research and legal cases indicates, then matching by scores is also skewed. The real cause of the gender gap is bias in the test: despite the fact that they receive better grades in high school and college in comparable classes, females receive lower scores on the SAT. This remains true even when course taking patterns and course difficulty are accounted for. The test-maker has been unable to adequately account for this discrepancy, but independent research shows that the timed, multiple-choice format of the exams, the roles of females in test questions, the penalty for guessing, and "stereotype bias" may all play roles in artificially depressing females' test scores.

Myth #7. Test coaching doesn't work to improve SAT scores
Studies collected by Fair Test show that good coaching programs can raise a student's scores by 100 points or more. Many of these courses are very expensive ($800 and up), and teach little more than test-taking strategies specific to the SAT. The fact that short-term coaching works undermines the test-makers' claim that the SAT measures skills and knowledge learned over a long period of time. It also adds another income-related bias to the test, since students who come from families that can afford an expensive coaching class are already more likely to score higher on the test. Moreover, why do both ETS and the College Board sell test preparation products if coaching doesn't work?

Myth #8. Bias reduction techniques guarantee that the test is fair
Whatever else their procedures may be doing, they are not eliminating bias from the test. ETS' own research indicates that the overall format of the test itself is to blame. The SAT is a fast-paced, multiple-choice test which rewards strategic guessing -- a non-academic skill at which males tend to excel. The methods used to screen individual test items for bias, such as "differential item functioning," fail to eliminate large discrepancies between students of different racial groups. One analysis of the October 1998 SAT showed that out of 78 Verbal and 60 Math questions, there were no items on which African Americans or Chicanos outperformed Whites.

Myth #9. The SAT is needed to counteract grade inflation
No definitive proof exist showing that grade inflation is running rampant throughout U.S. high schools, as many in the testing industry claim. Even if one assumes that grades are going up at a much faster rate than test scores, this trend would be a rising tide that

lifts all boats. Applicants can still be accurately compared with one another since everyone's grades would be increasing and rank-in-class does not change.

Myth #10. The SAT measures what you need to know in college
The SAT is a mind game that has nothing to do with skills necessary for higher education: it tests a tiny range of techniques, mainly how quickly you can choose among four or five answers without thinking deeply about any of them. For example, research shows that over 40% of reading comprehension items can be answered correctly without reading the passage. Some of the many qualities you need in college that the SAT cannot measure are writing ability, strategic reasoning, higher order thinking skills, experience, persistence and creativity.

Chapter 32 - Keeping you from Handling your Business

GMAT Basics:

The Graduate Management Admissions Test is the standardized exam used by graduate business schools for admissions decisions. It is designed and produced by the Educational Testing Service (ETS) and administered through the Graduate Management Admissions Council (GMAC). The three-hour, computer-adaptive test is almost exclusively multiple-choice and GMAC has been able to validate the GMAT for just one purpose: predicting first-year graduate school grades. But GMAC concedes that the GMAT can predict less than 17% of the variation in these grades on average. Independent researchers put the percentage much lower at between 41 points before they indicate a difference in the abilities measured by the GMAT which means that colleges cannot determine the better qualified of two students whose scores are 530 and 570.

Admissions Cutoff Scores:

Due to the GMAT's weak validity and lack of precision, the GMAC Code of Ethics states: "Avoid the use of cutoff scores. Cutoff scores should only be used when there is clear empirical evidence that a large proportion of the applicants scoring below the cutoff scores have substantial difficulty doing satisfactory graduate work. GMAC continues, "In addition, it is incumbent upon the school to demonstrate that the use of cutoff scores does not result in the systematic exclusion of members of either sex, any age or ethnic groups, or any other relevant groups in the face of other evidence that would indicate their competence or predict their success." In addition, the National Association of Graduate Admissions Professionals' handbook Professional Standards and Practices states, "It is advisable to consider implementation of additional practices that eliminate discrimination, provide equal access and treat tests as a single component of the admissions procedure since test scores are not the sole measure of potential success."

Despite this strong guidance, hundreds of schools use absolute cutoff scores for admission and financial aid. For example, Texas Christian University has an accelerated MBA program that requires a 620 on the GMAT. Chapman College of Business and Concordia University each demand a 500, while California State University at Stanlihaus mandates a 450. The University of North Florida is even more explicit: "a minimum 20 verbal and 22 quantitative GMAT sub-score is required for graduate admission."

GMAC recognizes these abuses are widespread, noting among "Business School Application Tips" in one publication, "Minimum Score Requirements: Some schools require minimum scores on the Graduate Management Admission GMAT. Other schools only have minimum requirements for certain sections of the GMAT. Know the minimum requirement at a particular school, if one exists, so you only apply to schools you are qualified to attend."

GMAC takes no action against schools that misuse its test results. In fact, schools with cutoff scores are listed in GMAC's college search and financial aid identification programs and given all of the benefits of GMAC membership.

GMAT "Merit" Scholarships:

Millions of dollars in "merit" scholarships are based on GMAT cutoff scores. For example, the University of Oregon's Lundquist College of Business Scholarship requires a 650 on the GMAT. Many aid programs consider only the GMAT "Total" score (Verbal + Quantitative), potentially decreasing the number of women by excluding Analytic Writing.

The average cost to attend business school is a little over $10,000 per year. Top 25 schools however, cost more than double that, potentially pricing out many of the 95% of Black and 80+% of Latino test-takers who report they need financial aid. In contrast, Whites are least likely to need aid but most likely to get it from GMAT score-based "merit" scholarships.

Business School Rankings and the GMAT:

Rankings publicized by magazines such as U. S. News & World Report and Business Week contribute to the illusion that GMAT scores are a valid measure of the worth of graduate management programs and their students. The average GMAT scores of enrolled students count for almost one-sixth of a school's total weight in both publications. Nearly a quarter of all MBA applicants say these rankings are "extremely important" for deciding where to apply. Many business schools point to rising scores as evidence of higher standards, neglecting to put them in the context of the rapid climb of average GMAT scores -- 57 points in the past 18 years.

AVERAGE GMAT TOTAL SCORES 2000 - 2001*

*most recent year data is available

All Test-takers	527
Women	503
Men	541
Whites	538
Blacks	427
Latinos	451-474 (several nationalities)

Test Coaching Distorts Scores:

GMAT preparation courses from firms such as Princeton Review and Kaplan promise to raise scores by an average of 92 points for those who can afford $800 to $1000 or more. Thousands of college graduates eagerly shell out millions of dollars every year to these companies. Business school admissions offices have no way to tell which applicants have been coached and which have not been.

Women and the MBA:

Women graduate from college with higher undergraduate Grade Point Averages (GPAs) than men but score 38 points lower on the GMAT- - a gap that has grown by 28 points since 1982. Women who graduate from Business School have, on average, GPA's equivalent to those of men. Independent research indicates that the GMAT over-predicts the performance of men and under-predicts that of women.

Test scores play a role in school choice. Men are much more likely than women to send their GMAT reports to "Top 20" schools and define such a school as their top preference. Women submit fewer applications and apply to less selective schools than their male counterparts.

The number of women in business schools peaked at 30% and remained flat for several years. GMAC reports that while 87% of MBA programs received more total applications for 2001-2002, less than half of these schools saw an increase in applications from women. Almost one-third of business schools at private universities have seen a drop in female applicants.

African Americans and Latinos:
In 2000-2001 African Americans scored, on average, 111 points lower than Whites. Latino populations scored between 64 and 87 points lower than Whites. The huge score gap between Blacks and Whites has narrowed only slightly in two decades, while the difference between Latinos and Whites has widened.

In 1994-1995 only 143 Blacks scored higher than 650 (over 100 points lower than the averages for top-tier schools). High-scoring Whites outnumbering high- scoring Blacks 75 to 1. Without affirmative action, African Americans and Hispanics would be much less likely to get into a top-25 graduate business school.

Members of these groups enter the MBA pipeline with far more concerns regarding their abilities to meet academic and curriculum demands, fears reinforced by much lower GMAT scores. African Americans and Hispanics are greatly disadvantaged by a test with little predictive ability and multiple opportunities for abuse.

Other Groups:
Applicants who speak English as a second language (ESL) are disadvantaged by the primarily multiple-choice nature of the GMAT and the fast pace at which items must be answered. ETS studies show that when these characteristics are not part of the test (as in the Analytic Writing section) the score gap between whites and ESL applicants is greatly reduced.
GMAC admits that average scores decline for test-takers over the age of 31. There is also an inverse relationship between GMAT scores and business experience. Studies conducted for GMAC show GMAT scores under-predict the performance of older students (particularly women) but demonstrate that business experience directly contributes to success in MBA programs.

While little research has been done on the validity of GMAT scores for students with disabilities, the test is likely to have the same discriminatory impact and low predictive validity as similar standardized admission tests produced by ETS such as the SAT.

Alternatives:
GMAC and ETS have long been the national gatekeepers for business school admissions. Soon there might be some competition. Researchers at the University of Michigan's School of Business have developed alternative measures of managerial potential that they claim better predict success in both academic and practical endeavors. This new assessment approach, dubbed the "Rainbow Project," also claims to produce far less racial and gender bias than the GMAT.

In 1985 Harvard Business School (HBS) decided to eliminate the GMAT from their admissions process. John Lynch, the Admissions Director at the time, gave several compelling reasons. In a blind test, Harvard found that admissions decisions made with and without the GMAT were essentially the same. Success at Harvard depended on intangibles such as motivation, interpersonal skills, perseverance and hard work – all factors not measured by GMAT. Looking at undergraduate grade-point average (UGPA), ethics, leadership, community activities, prior work experience and the interview made GMAT scores "superfluous". Harvard was also concerned about the perceived emphasis applicants place on the GMAT and that strong applicants with scores below the 99th percentile were intimidated from applying. Lynch also pointed out that an "artificial barrier to the admission of qualified but poorer students is unacceptable."

Eleven years later Harvard reinstated the GMAT, saying the decision "reflects the fact that there have been significant improvements to the structure of the test". The only changes made since 1954 have been the addition of the AWA, which is used only sporadically and the move to the Computer Adaptive Test, which came with multiple problems. Harvard also pledged to work closely with GMAC to cooperate "on ways to further change the test" to focus on intangible qualities. In six years, no further mention has been made of changes to the test.

Now, the pages you have been waiting for- What strategies could turn things around.

Section 3: The Principles

Chapter 33 - Work While Its Day

Many of the problems that plague minorities is their income rarely exceeds the minimum needed to meet their obligations. They are either underemployed or underpaid. These groups have rested their hopes on substantial raises and promotions that would finally give them the resources to make ends meet and even purchase some of the things they have longed to have for many years. The fact is, these bonuses and promotions rarely come or when they do come, it is either late in arriving or short-lived. Instead of relying on the inevitable disappointment, change the focus and return to what made survival in America possible from the first day your ancestors arrived. Look for multiple jobs that can provide multiple streams of income. Look for that second job, enter into job sharing opportunities and take advantage of existing skills and talent.

A few years ago my son, could not hold down a full time summer job because of his participation in college athletics. During his first year in school, we wondered why he never needed any money when he came home or when we would ask him over the phone. During a visit over the holidays, we finally discovered his personal survival strategy. While in high school, my son became very proficient at cutting his own hair and the heads of his teammates. Shortly after arriving at the college, he was inundated with request from friends and acquaintances that learned by observation and word of mouth that he was able to keep their heads looking good. Some of his customers had the audacity to call him late at night nearly every weekend in advance of the weekend parties. In an attempt to seize the opportunity, carve out some down time for himself and prevent some from taking advantage of him, he began to charge five dollars for each cut. With the right price, a captured customer base and a friendly disposition, he managed to make hundreds of dollars to keep money in his pocket and gas in his car.

After the recent presidential election, my son used some of that downtime to create an impressive piece of artwork commemorating the historic election. With obvious pride and humility, he showed me his artwork and asked me what I thought of the piece. Immediately, I saw the hidden potential in the piece, praised him for his talent and posed a business proposition. I informed him, that with a little bit of thought he could turn this into passive income for many years to come. The entire family (my daughter was finishing her marketing degree, my wife had one of the largest networks in the city and I was always looking for opportunities to use my own MBA skills) rallied around him and came up with a marketing and pricing plan. Within a few months, he had sold over 500 prints and earned thousands in profits with little effort. His "downtime art" was now registered in the Library of Congress and sitting in living rooms from Hawaii to Pennsylvania and at least two foreign countries. He also, had produced a companion print that would nearly double his revenues by the end of the year!

This type of success has not been unusual for our family. Through the years, our desire and need for additional income has resulted in other profitable and not so profitable ventures. While seating on my front porch with friends and pontificating about goals and plans, I breathed words that I did not even know were in my heart. I told my unsuspecting friends and myself that I wanted to open and run a Christian Bookstore. I did not have the means nor the knowledge to make the idea a reality. But from that day, the thought never left me and the desire became stronger. I was confident that the thought and desire came from above. Shortly, after entering my MBA program, I began to learn things that made the dream more of a possibility. Week after week, the burning desire to fulfill the dream drove me to do the necessary research, planning and networking to help make it a reality. Seven years after the words crossed my lips I opened my on line Christian bookstore, was setting appointments with clients and booking my first contracts. I had a simple marketing strategy; provide the same products and services while passing on much of the discounts to the churches who were my primary customers. My research had shown that the current companies were subjecting these same churches to huge price markups in order to stay in business. I ran the business for more than five years with varying degrees of success. I eventually had to scale back my operations because of consolidation in the market, restrictions on loans and unfair trade practices that prevented online booksellers from gaining the same discounts and access to products as brick and mortar stores. Nevertheless, for several years I was able to make money and help churches make the most of their funds at the same time.

Chapter 34 - The Bugatti Principle: Some one always has something better

Recently, a world famous singer purchased one of the most expensive production cars in the world for her husband. Shortly after I heard about the purchase, I happened to catch a special on the Discovery channel that showed how these cars were made. I was astonished to learn that this car cost approximately $1 million to make and took over six months to manufacture. The cost to replace the tires on the vehicle exceeded $15,000! I must admit the car was truly amazing and would probably be a blast to drive. However, watching the program made me more aware of a simple fact that whatever you obtain someone will always have something better.

Unfortunately, most people live as if they are totally oblivious to this simple truth. They constantly seek to gain something that will provide some measure of self-esteem or superiority over their neighbor or peers. That expensive automobile that no one else in the neighborhood has is suddenly the most important goal to achieve. Also, every moment of conversation is spent talking about how wonderful the car is and how great the car feels to drive. Even worse, some of them make claims of how "The car is a Blessing from God" and shows how much "God favors them." This mentality leads people to purchase every thing from homes to jewelry to furniture and phones all in the name of favor with an underlying motive of covetousness and pride. The financial toll of such poor judgment is staggering. If this describes you, I urge you to begin to think and act differently. If you don't think anything is wrong with this way of living that's okay but you don't have to join them.

Everyone who brags on his new Honda, Mercedes, BMW, Lexus or even Bugatti are in self-delusion. Why? Because, someone else rolled out of the car lot with the same or better vehicle with more options and features. Every person that flaunts an expensive watch or ring fails to realize that the overpriced piece of jewelry might as well be costume jewelry in the eyes of the truly wealthy. The point is, every attempt to flaunt your wealth or to pretend to flaunt wealth is nothing but vanity and a losing game. Here is what I suggest:

Those who dwell in the lowest two income categories should never seek to purchase a new vehicle using their operating income. That is, income that you need to live from month to month. Instead, purchase a well maintained used vehicle from a company that has a history of long term quality. Don't be deceived by the commercials that tout "best in initial quality." This is just marketing speak for "this car will disappoint you after two years of use." It doesn't matter if it is made in America or not, what does matter is its ability to stay on the American roads for years.

If individuals in the lower two income brackets do happen to fall into expendable resources (expendable to me means I will not need this money in the next five years to survive or make my payments), they should be realistic when they purchase a new vehicle. Keep the same principles of longevity and value in mind. Also, do not over buy! Use this rule of thumb: Spend no more than 80% of the money you were going to use to purchase the car and save the balance to pay for the maintenance and other expenses of the vehicle. Also consider how you will pay for regular maintenance when that 20% is gone. Will your salary and budget cover paying ¼ of the money you set aside at any one time?

These rules also apply to those in the third and fourth income categories if they do not have sufficient reserve funds especially when it comes to not over buying. Even if you can comfortably afford a new vehicle, don't lose your mind. That luxury car, no matter how grand, flashy or fast, will still only get you from point A to B within the confines of the local speed limits. If you do have a taste for extravagance and the ordinary just will not do, consider maxing out the options on a premium car versus buying the bottom line luxury car. Do not get suckered in to buying a luxury car with standard features when you can pick and choose the options that will really get your motor running. This will save you from paying (probably with interest) for options that you rarely use. You also avoid the high maintenance fees that come with the luxury vehicle.

The Bugatti principle can be applied to nearly every major purchase that you make. That 63 inch Flat panel TV in your den has already been trumped by someone's 70 inch model on the next block. And, instead of paying that high price, you could have gotten an "out of the box" or "closeout" model for 20-50% less if you had only shopped around. For you jewelry buffs who can't stay away from the huge stones, you could save your self some buyer's remorse buy adhering to this principle as well.

Chapter 35 - The Alarm Clock Principle

When I was in high school several decades ago, I was given an alarm clock. This cheap, non-descript alarm clock served two purposes; it kept me abreast of the time and was very effective in waking me up for school, church and work. I would not be lying if I shared that it made the most annoying sound possible when the current time matched the alarm setting. My girlfriend, fiancé and wife (all the same person) literally hated the nerve-shredding alarm for most of those years that it sat on my dresser. But, over the course of nearly fifteen years it never failed to wake me up. And after we were married, she was awoken from the deepest sleep every time the last second before the buzzer elapsed. It wasn't until this constant nightly companion lost its voice (the buzzer broke) that I had to reluctantly purchase another alarm clock. Although we purchased a more modern and neatly sounding clock, my wife and I both lamented the demise of our former electronic rooster.

You may be begging for me to get to the point and I will right now. No matter what you have purchased, have been given or has happen to come into your possession, if it works don't be quick to get rid of it. For nearly fifteen years while I was benefitting from my simple alarm clock, companies were making, marketing and selling "better and more stylish" alarm clocks. Every time I received a paycheck or monetary gift I could have been tempted to buy one of these newer models. For the years when my wife was complaining about the annoying buzzer I was often tempted to discard what was effectively serving both of us and pursue an alternative that couldn't possibly do a better job.

As a young mechanical engineering student, one of the first design principles I learned was that "form always follows function". This means that the primary thing I needed to focus on was making sure that the machine or equipment worked as designed. How the finished product looked was secondary. The vanity of appearance never made the design better in and of itself. We have to be willing to apply this principle to everything that we own. Let's learn how to hold on to the things we know are getting the job done. This will allow us to hold on to the money we would have spent unnecessarily. If you have a watch, pair of shoes, sofa, car, stove, etc, that still works fine, resist the temptation to turn it in for the "latest and greatest" model. Before you make the decision to replace that item ask yourself these critical questions: Is what I have now still performing the function it was intended to perform? Is what I have now costing me less money than it would cost to purchase and maintain the replacement? Am I considering the replacement because I want to keep up with my neighbors/peers? Unless you can honestly and objectively answer "no" to all three questions, you should question if you are ready to make the purchase.

Chapter 36 - The 2 for 1 principle – share apartments, homes, anything you can...

During my nearly four decades of living in America, I have been able to witness how most of the ethnic groups live and survive. Each group seems to have crafted unique strategies for handling the challenges faced by those who are looking up at the American Dream. These may not always seem logical to others and may even seem strange to most. I have even heard other groups say things like, "There is no way I could ever do that!" But what I have never heard is someone say that these strategies are ineffective or worthless. In a recent trip to Dallas, I saw a news report where certain immigrants were found living 50 plus in a single family home. It was obvious that they were using the home as a resting place. There were sleeping bags everywhere as well as food and trash. This style of communal living is popular among immigrant groups who are trying to save money to establish themselves in America. Some of them have multiple families living in housing that many of us would consider too small for ourselves.

You can also find many of these immigrants riding five to a car to work every day and typically driving an older model car that they probably brought with cash. These same immigrants also bring their lunches to work or share lunches to save money. Making a trip to their homes also reveals an unexpected level of frugality in home decor and furnishings that are unexpected. Likewise, there is a modest approach to clothing, make-up and other adornments. It appears that they are laser focused on saving money and making the most of their opportunity in America.

What can "native" minorities learn from these examples? Certainly, I am neither condoning nor advocating that minority groups give up all that they know and love to live like immigrants. That would be no more successful than encouraging them to mirror the habits of the majority group. However, I am imploring these groups to rethink the way they do everything. It is imperative that strategies and approaches need to be explored and tried that will improve their ability to make the most of the opportunity into which they were born. Is this far-fetched or asking for too much? I think not. All that has to be done is to reach back into their collective memories and remember how struggles were conquered in the past.

Minority groups have never fully been credited with some very clever inventions solely birthed out of the need for survival. During the civil rights struggle of the 50's and 60's, cakes and pies were sold to fund the movement as workers boycotted their employers and bus lines and required other means of getting around town. Rent parties were a product of lean times in tenement housing as families struggled to keep roofs over their heads. I remember my dad working extra hours and routes to account for boxes of chickens and vegetables he gave to relatives that were struggling to feed their large families. I also remember moving in with my parents and mother-in-law, respectively to save the money for the down payments for two of the homes we have purchased. In any event, minorities have to take it to the next level, swallow any pride that has built up and do what is necessary to be successful.

Chapter 37 - The "3-more years" Strategy- Don't kick those kids out at 18

One of the most devastating mindsets that many minorities in America have is in the way they perceive the maturation process. This is true for both parents and the children they raise. It is not uncommon to hear parents say things like, "I can't wait to this child turns 18 they are getting out of this house.!" Likewise, their children are itching to get away from their parents' home and the rules that have steered their lives since birth. Unfortunately, neither the parents nor the children have a solid plan for what happens on the day after they part company. It is as if they expect some magical thing to occur that will ensure that the child will quickly mature and gain the ability to make the critical decisions required to survive. It is the classic "sink or swim" philosophy, applied in a situation that leads to more sinking children than strong swimmers. Of course the parents and children have selfish motives that serve as detriments to the generational success of their families.

First, eighteen years of sacrifice on anything should not be followed by a misguided decision aimed at regaining long lost freedom. It is akin to working at a job you loved for many years and retiring the first day you are eligible never considering what you will do with yourself or account for the lost resources and income. Such people hope they can still pay the bills, eat well and take care of medical expenses that will undoubtedly happen sooner or later. For the children, their unbridled enthusiasm about leaving home leaves them blind to the impending struggles for finding stable housing and employment. They also have no idea of the true cost of liberty and independence. If you are one of those anxious teenagers, understand that you are about to throw away the most stable thing you have known since leaving the womb.

Parents should sit down with their teens and develop a plan for the transition to adulthood. The years between 16 and 21 are arguably the most important for the maturation process and economic stability of our children. Critical decisions regarding education, job potential and house rules need to be discussed openly and honestly. Dropping out of high school should never be an option regardless of the circumstances. Is work or college the most viable option at the moment? What career options are realistic? What jobs are currently in high demand or will be in demand once the child is ready? These decisions should be made with realistic expectations.

When I was in the ninth grade, the school had the students take an assessment test that was supposed to indicate the careers that best fit your skills and talents. At the beginning of the test, I was asked to select three fields that interested me the most. Since I had not given it a great deal of thought, I put down some of the usual choices: Doctor, Lawyer and Engineer. After taking the test we received the results a few weeks later in our homeroom classes. Surprisingly, the test indicated that I had the abilities required to be successful at any of the three.

Now the tough choices had to be made. Which of these careers would I pursue? What path presented the most reasonable possibility of leading to a successful career? It would be nice to say that I took my own advice and sat down with my parents to determine what would be the best choice for me. Unfortunately, I can't make that claim, but I did as much soul searching as a 15 year old is capable of doing to determine my decision. My logic went something like this: Becoming a Doctor would take as much as twelve years of schooling. I wasn't sure if I was up for that much schooling and I was definitely sure that my parents couldn't afford to pay for it anyway. I also recognized that becoming a lawyer required a ton of reading that I was not very fond of during the nine plus years of schooling that was already under my belt. Also, extemporaneous speaking (this phrase was not part of my vocabulary in the ninth grade) and debating were not my strong suits. However, I was very good at math, loved science and was pretty curious about how things worked. Add to this a decent ability to draw and an honorable mention in the school's science fair made engineering the logical choice. At that time, I spent nearly all of my free time drawing, creating or using math to capture statistics on my electric football set. I had several different teams that I played against each other and kept statistics on every offensive player. This was well before the days of the modern video systems, so I did all of the calculations by hand. I didn't even have a calculator.

Once the decision was made to pursue mechanical engineering, I shared it with my very supportive parents. I would need this support as I pursued this dream of becoming the first professional in my families history. First, I elected to pack as much science, technical drawing and math into my high school curriculum as possible to best prepare me for college. This decision was made by me without my guidance counselor, but I needed her help to figure out how to make it a reality. I won't bore you with the details of the courses I had to take, but it was a grueling schedule that cost me in more than one way. I had to take my gym classes during the summer breaks because I did not have room for them during the regular school year. My parents had to pay for these courses and while my friends were enjoying their summers or working, I was running and baking under the summer sun. Also, the heavy schedule of advanced placement courses took a toll on my GPA and class ranking. I finished just out of the top ten in class rank and missed the National Honor Society by 1/100th of a point. However, I did get acceptance letters from an Ivy League school, the best university in my state and several scholarships to these and other very good schools. Also, when my friends were struggling with college calculus, I was making all A's in my required two years. I was fortunate enough to spend thirteen years as a mechanical and nuclear engineer prior to moving on to financial services.

Chapter 38 - The "29ᵗʰ Day" Principle

Imagine for a few moments that you owned a lovely little cottage home that provided scenic views of a beautiful pond that was always bursting with life. For as long as you've known you have spent mornings and late afternoons admiring the wild life that seems to thrive in this scenic environment. One morning while finishing your favorite morning beverage you notice something that in your recollection you have never seen. A single lily pad has appeared on the surface of the pond. The next morning while collecting the remnants of your breakfast, you notice there are now two lily pads floating in the water. In fact, everyday that follows leads you to conclude that the number of lily pads are growing almost exponentially.

One afternoon, you get an unexpected visit from a dear friend (who just happens to be a botanist). Your friend notices the lily pad phenomenon and asks one simple question, "How long has it been since you saw the first lily pad?" You respond with a not so certain, "I believe it has been about 29 days, Why?" He informs you that unless something is done quickly your beloved pond is doomed. He goes on to say that by this time tomorrow your beloved pond will be filled with lily pads. At that point, the lily pads will begin to rapidly deplete the life giving oxygen from the pond. Soon after, everything associated with the pond will begin to suffocate and die.

Unfortunately, you find it hard to accept your friends devastating prognosis. How could your pond be dying or virtually dead already? The birds are still chirping, the surrounding trees and bushes are as green as ever and there is no sign of stress in the fish. Also, in spite of the large number of lily pads, there is still so much open surface on the pond! As a result you politely thank your friend for his concern and choose to offer another beverage instead of inquiring about what to do next.

For those who do not know, this previous story is a personal adaptation of an old riddle I am using to teach the devastating impact of procrastination. Many people and especially those in the most vulnerable segments of our society are living and spending like they have all of the time in the world. They are making decisions day after day seemingly totally oblivious to the impending doom. They find various ways to rationalize their financial decisions always believing that they have plenty of time to recover.

However, most of them are already on Day 29 and minutes from Day 30. Like the fish freely sucking up the seemingly endless oxygen on Day 29 and 30, these free spenders can't imagine an end to the funds and credit that makes their current lives possible. Unless changes are made quickly, the irreversible affects of the decisions will soon find them gasping during the final breaths of their financially devastated lives. The moral of this story is that no matter what stage of life you are in it is important to remember that time is rarely ever your friend!

Chapter 39 - "Micro-Credit" principle" – Use the small credit you can get to your own benefit. Also learn to help each other

A truly amazing phenomenon that is helping many of the world's poorest citizens reach a level of success that rises above their wildest imaginations. The concept of Micro-loans have allowed industrious and hard-working entrepeneurs start their own businesses. With seed money of as little as a few hundred dollars they are able to purchase the needed goods or supplies to create products they can sell at a substantial profit. Many of these unlikely small business owners quickly pay back their loans and become self-sufficient. With a small leg up they are able to move forward and create that once unattainable future for themselves and their families.

This small example brings into focus two key concepts; do not despise small beginnings and everyone's little can become much when it is used collectively and with the right intentions. First, remember that the journey to the top starts with the smallest of steps. If you can't get that big loan you think you need to start your business, figure out what you can do with the small finances you can obtain. If you have a small amount of money to invest and can't meet the minimum the investment companies are looking for, look for other legal means of turning it into a reasonable profit.

Let me give a small example. Suppose you had $500 sitting in your savings account and not needed to take care of any pending obligations. Leaving the money sitting in that account for twelve months at today's interest rates may net you a whopping $2.50 cents in interest income. Now suppose while your money is sitting there making the bank much more money, your friends are struggling to make ends meet, paying bills and keeping a roof over their heads. One day, while hearing about their problems, a blinking neon sign goes off in your head saying you can make a difference and small profit at the same time. You decide to make a micro-loan to your friend in need with simple terms of $500 today for $505 on next payday! By so doing, you can make as much interest in one month as you would have made the entire year. And, if you decide to continue to do this each month with other friends and acquaintances to meet various financial needs you can turn that $5 into $60. Instead of a miserly 0.25% interest you can have a healthy and enviable 12% return on your investment.

Perhaps, you might think that you are risking your $500 in such one time, single point transactions. Well, you can mitigate that risks by making smaller loans for the same or higher profit margin. For instance, five $100 dollar loans with $1 or $2 "signs of appreciation" on payday will spread out the risk and produce the same result. However, such actions accomplish more than increase your amount of interest. It meets the needs of people who would not otewise get help. It keeps money in the community that would otherwise go to big corporations in the form of late and penalty fees. It may help a struggling business stay afloat and keep somebody employed at least for another day. And the most important benefit is that you are taking matters into your own hands and doing what is necessary to improve your financial condition on your own terms.

Chapter 40 - Home Sweet Home- Not really Principle

One prevailing thought is that "buying" a home is the best thing that a person can do to be prosperous in America. Not much could be further from the truth. In reality purchasing a home without paying cash for it is not much different than renting. The common way homes are purchased in America involve saving for a down payment, finding a home (with or without the assistance of a real estate agent), finding a financial institution willing to loan the money for the purchase, getting the required insurance and signing up for a long term commitment to faithfully pay your new silent and invisible co-tenets, also known as the bank and city government.

Traditionally, this arrangement has almost always appeared to work out to the benefit of the buyer. The home had a reasonable chance of growing in value, the homeowner benefited from tax breaks associated with interest and taxes and when the time came to sell could expect to recover the down payment. With a proposition like that mortgage companies, real estate agents, builders and developers had an easy job of convincing more than eager buyers to jump on board. However, this model was all but blown to bits with the recent crash of the housing market.

The housing market crash should have turned upside down every assumption people believed about the value of purchasing a mortgage to own a home. I say 'should' because the marketers of the status quo are still peddling the same rhetoric and products only with a new package. They are encouraging unsophisticated homeowners and would be homeowners to refinance or purchase homes like nothing happened. In fact, their new motto is: "there has never been a better time" to make that purchase.

Here is the reality that has been ignored for years but has never been truer since the housing market collapse. There is actually little difference between rental leasing and mortgages when housing prices are rising very slowly, stagnant, or falling. Instead of entering into the standard one year lease, the homeowner has entered into a 15 or 30 year lease with the only option for early termination being a successful sale of the home. In lieu of making a nominal security deposit of the first and last months rent, the homeowner offers up a non-refundable security deposit equivalent to a minimum of 5% of the purchase price. That "deposit" has grown to as much as 20% since the mortgage crisis! In addition to paying the mortgage "rent" on time, the mortgagee promises to pay other monthly, quarterly or yearly fees such as insurance (flood and homeowners'), real estate taxes and association dues. But, unlike a renter, the mortgagee must pay all of the utilities, fix anything that breaks and maintain the lawn!

One could argue that even though the homeowner has to pay out more each month, they still have the advantage and exclusive privileges not available to the renter. These would be tangible things like tax breaks on interest paid and intangible things like privacy and space. However, the renter can obtain much of the tax break by giving an equivalent amount to charity. Which would you prefer to do; give to a program that helps needy people or give hundreds of dollars each month to a 'not so needy' financial institution!?

Chapter 41 - Don't be "Unequally Yoked" Principle

Bible believing Christians or avid bible readers know exactly what comes to mind when they hear the phrase "Unequally Yoked". However, for those who are not as familiar with the bible let me spend a few lines getting you on the same page. In the Bible verse 2 Corinthians 6:14, the Apostle Paul encourages the believers to avoid becoming unequally yoked with unbelievers. The phrase refers to a pair of oxen pulling a plow. In order to get the maximum work out of the oxen, the pair should be of equal size, strength, maturity and temperament. They must pull in tandem and unison to break up the fallow ground, create straight rows and prevent breaking the plow.

He understood and wanted them to recognize that living a life of a Christian would be infinitely harder when you are married to someone living in opposition to the teachings of Christ. In such relationships, every decision made and every situation faced represents an opportunity for heartache, struggle and ungodly compromise. Unfortunately, this goes beyond the spiritual aspects of their lives. It also can be directly applied to the way money management occurs in the relationship. In other words, being unequally yoked financially can be devastating and will cripple your potential economic future. A home that contains only one partner focused on money management, prudent purchasing and financial discipline is a difficult and tenable situation.

Consider a situation in which two people who are equally accountable and responsible for their survival must cross a desert to get to a lush green valley. You might even want to imagine that they are connected together by invisible handcuffs or ankle chains that make it impossible for the actions and movements of one to not affect the other. Understanding the difficulty of the journey ahead, one partner has carefully planned for the refreshing water, nourishing food and adequate shelter needed to survive. The diligent partner has also attempted to share the plans and details of the provisions made to the barely interested partner. In contrast, the other partner doesn't actively participate in the planning, is unaware of the provisions needed and has a naive view of the dangers lurking ahead. From the inception of the journey, the maladjusted partner is not focused on preserving the critical resources and constantly complains about the size of the rations. In fact, what the prudent partner doesn't know is that the uncooperative partner has hidden and is consuming resources that were set aside in secret. Moreover, at every critical moment on the journey, the weak link of a partner is ready to give up or complaining that they have not yet gotten to the intended destination. All of this makes for an arduous, and emotional draining journey that is bound to end in disaster.

I recognize that it is easy to dismiss this as an impossible and unlikely abstraction from reality. However, I am convinced that this is playing out in many homes in America when it comes to managing finances. Even more likely, is the impact that such behavior is having on minority households across the country. The groups that can least afford financial disharmony are experiencing it just as frequently as everyone else.

Let me provide a practical example that played out in front of my wife and I several years ago. At this time in our lives my wife and I were working full time jobs and raising our two children. My wife came to me with an idea. She was considering taking a part time job at a clothing store near our home. Her logical argument was that she really liked the clothing line in this store and she could use the extra money and store discount to pay for her purchases that she would be making from this store anyway.

As if I really had a decision to make, I accepted her logic and agreed that it would be a good thing for her because she had a good eye for fashion. On the evenings she worked, I would often pick her up to ensure she was safe and felt comfortable closing the store. On one particular occasion, I was waiting in the car for her to end her shift when I noticed a young couple drive into the parking lot and stopped in the front of the store.

As the car came to a stop, I could not help but notice that the driver was not very happy. In fact, he looked very angry and upset. When the car stopped, the young lady got out of the car, opened the back door and grabbed several items of clothing. From my vantage point, I could see that her hair was in disarray, the dress she was wearing was torn and her makeup followed the tracks of what were tears streaming down her face. After grabbing the clothes she quickly entered the store as her companion sat in silence seemingly staring straight ahead. After she returned to the car, they calmly drove away. I do not believe I ever saw this couple again, but they left an indelible impression on me.

When my wife's shift ended and she got into the car with me, I couldn't help but ask what happened when the young lady came into the store. She told me that the young lady came into the store very apologetic and requested permission to return the items she just purchased. She explained that she and her husband had gotten into a fight because he was not pleased with the amount of money she had been spending on clothes. By the way, the store had a "no refund" policy that was to be strictly enforced. That meant exchanges or store credit only and only if you have a receipt. Since the woman left without any clothes, the store manager either made an exception or gave her store credit.

My wife went on to say how horrible her husband was to treat her this way! Although I agreed with her, I took the worst time to turn this into one of those teachable moments. I mistakingly shared that I could also understand why he was upset! Not understanding that I needed to quickly change the subject, I went on to say that this man could have been trying for months to communicate to his wife about the level of spending that was going on and how it was affecting their home. Perhaps, he ran out of ways to get his point across or really did not know how to express his position in an articulate way. Whatever the situation was, his frustration led him to believe he had run out of options.

I clearly stated that I did not agree with the option this young man took at all. Nevertheless, my loose tongue and dimwitted comments led to one of the biggest arguments that my wife and I have ever had. It was so painful, I believe I have consciously erased the details from my memory. But, I do remember that we agreed to disagree because there was no true common ground. The only thing that it did was begin to highlight the differences in our ideals and philosophies regarding the use of money and family finances.

You might be tempted to say, "Not me!" or "Not Us!" But consider the following before you finish your personal introspection. If you or your partner have ever purchased something and hid it from the other knowing that they would be upset because of your current financial situation, you might be unequally yoked. If either you or your partner have gotten upset, nervous or started an argument intentionally when it came time to discuss the family budget, you may be unequally yoked. If you get depressed, upset or seriously disappointed because you can't spend money when and how much you want, you may be unequally yoked! If you and your partner can't agree on how much to spend on special events like christmas, anniversaries and birthdays, you may be unequally yoked. Truthfully, there are a myriad of ways couples can be financially unequally yoked and you need to seriously explore how well matched you and your significant other are when it comes to finances.

You may be wondering, "What if we are unequally yoked? What, if anything can we do about that?" These are indeed tough questions involving a topic that has no easy solutions. However, there are some key things to keep in mind that will help you and your partner to respond appropriately. First, remember that it is nearly impossible for "leopards to change their spots." Spenders will always be spendthrifts at heart and no amount of intervention or conversation will cure them of that tendency. Next, financial counselors know money matters not matters of the heart or personal histories that have the most influence on how people view and use money. Also, no amount of income will make a person a good money manager, compensate for loose spending or make a tightwad feel good about unnecessary spending.

What you can do is live within the reality of your current situation. Spenders must be treated like potential addicts and loose money managers should be handled with nearly inflexible limits. Take away or limit their access to the excess cash or credit available to the home. However, tightwads need the equivalent of a security blanket or pacifier. Ensure them that whatever is done financially will not hinder paying the bills or reaching their ultimate savings goals. Both tactics require good, solid and constructive communication from both parties. Whenever you can't reach this level of communication just stop and vow to try again later when cooler heads and more open minds prevail.

Chapter 42 - Stop printing money!!

If you heard someone mention the phrase; "I wish they would stop printing money", you would probably think they were referring to the way the government handles its budget. Any time we get into a crisis the easiest thing for the government to do is print more paper and secure loans from foreign entities to cover them. We all understand the implications of this strategy, a short trip to a place of unmanageable debt and financial bondage. Unfortunately, our government may not learn its lesson until it is way too late.

However, you may not be aware of the fact that the government is not alone in its ability to "print more money". Every time anyone uses a credit card, buys something under credit terms, buys something over time (e.g. layaway plans), obtains and uses a line of credit they are essentially doing the same thing. They are printing and spending imaginary dollars today that they hope to back up with real dollars some time in the future. The problem is that those future dollars are almost always much more expensive. The hours that you have to work or the income that must be generated to produce the real dollars in the future are always more and harder to obtain. Future raises, bonuses and base salaries are barely enough to take care of the regular expenses that come due at the time that they are earned or received. Therefore, you can't and shouldn't bank on these future dollars to obtain items and things you want or need today. Of course, there are situations that will require "future dating" payment of expenses. But, please do so with caution, diligence and a full awareness of the cost. This is especially true for the financially disadvantaged.

Every person needs to understand that instruments like credit cards and lines of credit were originally introduced for the wealthy. They were designed to provide a convenience for those who already had plenty of money to meet their obligations and current needs or wants. Instead of having to trouble with writing a check or carrying around a lot of cash, it was much easier to hand someone this little plastic card that said payment in full will be made shortly thereafter. These were never meant for people whose only source of wealth was the paycheck coming at the end of the week nor for those who were only a few months of unpaid bills away from the poor house. Unfortunately, some purveyors of these products seized upon the opportunity to prey on the envies and lusts of the "have nots" towards the "haves" and found a way to make them available to the masses. These "financial tools" became so efficient at re-circulating our currency that our society found itself unable to imagine a financial system without widespread use of credit.

As for credit plans, rent-to-own dealers, pawn shops and layaways, these were especially designed for the financially disadvantaged. The purveyors of these products and services prey on the desperation and vulnerabilities of the poor. They position and peddle these products as either the last, only or best option for people with very limited resources. They tout themselves as the only companies really concerned about making your life better by providing a means of getting what you want. These wolves in sheep's clothing put together convincing ads (at times using celebrities) and easy approvals to ensure their teeth get sunk into your wallet or purse as deep as possible. Their true colors come out when the payment is late or missed or that wonderful piece of whatever no longer works.

I want to speak directly about layaways. I do not believe that all layaway programs are bad. In fact, those that allow you to spend money that you would have spent anyway over an extended period of time with no interest or penalty are actually great ways to budget. However, people make the mistake of purchasing more than they would have if they had all of the money at once. They also worsen their situation by spending more after the final payments are made. For instance, it is a good thing to start paying for an interest free Christmas layaway in September and finish paying for it at the beginning of December. However, it is a bad idea to take the next paycheck that should go toward bills and use it to buy a few more items to make Christmas "really" special.

Instead, plan your purchase and delay self-gratification until the time is right. Drop that pride and ask for a ride. Many folks would gladly provide transportation if you would be willing to pay even a fraction of what that car dealer is charging you to "Buy Here, Pay Here." Also, buy the things you can pay for right now. If that means you can only by one suit instead of two or purchase those shoes only in one color, make those simple choices. And, as you make these life-altering choices make sure you teach them to your children.

Chapter 43 - Money Does Grow on Trees

Ask anyone you meet have they heard of the phrase "Money doesn't grow on trees" and you would be hard-pressed to get anyone to say, "no!". Surprisingly, the full story on the origin of the famous proverb is not easy to pinpoint. The only thing I could discover is that the phrase may have originated in a newspaper article in 1820 at a time when paper money was just beginning to be widely used in America. The point being expressed in the article that it was tougher to get paper money than it was to get fruit from a tree.

Regardless of its origin or meaning, nearly every American is settled on the notion that wealth is hard to come by and even harder to accumulate. I really would like to use the familiarity of this axiom to drive home a key point: Money does grow on trees. However, the genome of the money tree is tied directly to your genealogical tree, that being your Family Tree. Money grows on Family Trees! It is a provable fact that nearly every wealthy and financially successful person in America and the world, gained a significant portion of their wealth from their ancestors. The implications of this truth are huge and can be expressed in five undeniable truths.

First, no one should expect the financial conditions of their progeny to vastly improve without providing something from which to build. Second, it is foolish for the financially disadvantaged to believe that wealth accumulation will come without extreme sacrifice and self-denial. Third, it is delusional for the economically deprived to believe that this time of sacrifice has an expiration date. Fourth, it is financial genocide for the poor to live a life that squanders any measure of wealth accumulated or handed down. Fifth, considering the depth of the economic hole or width of the wealth divide there is not a moment to waste. Lets take a closer look at each of these principles and determine how they translate into action.

The children need your help to begin their lives of independence and self-sufficiency. It is another provable fact that children of poor and disadvantaged minorities start off their adult working careers with much lower salaries and fewer financially helpful benefits. Add to that little to no credit and significant debt from seeking a higher level of education. Many of them struggle for decades if not all of their lives because they are forced to make it on their own. Any help provided by the parents can make this climb much more manageable. For my two children, we made a conscious decision to purchase good solid cars for them while they were in high school that we believed could last them well past college. We did not buy new vehicles, but we placed a standard for the age and condition of the vehicles. We searched far and wide for the best deal and made the sacrifice needed to pay for these vehicles ourselves. We also put in the money necessary to maintain these vehicles to increase the chances of them lasting as long as we hoped.

Another example of providing initial support was keeping our children on our auto insurance policies and paying the city taxes (yes, I live in a city that makes its residents pay personal property taxes) as long as they were driving these vehicles. A final example is the fact that we kept them on our family cell phone plan well into their adult years. They made the money to pay for their expensive smart phones and paid for the data plans each month, but did not have to pay the additional costs of a separate plan.

My wife and I are not rich by anyone's standards. Therefore, when it came time for our children to participate in character-building activities like sports, learning a musical instrument or going on a mission trip, we knew we had to "dig deep" to pay for these activities. That meant sacrificing many of the things we wanted to do or buy. Of course, we sought to make prudent decisions in the midst of providing these opportunities. For instance, when we believed the cost of AAU basketball outweighed the expected benefits we pulled our son out of the program. Likewise, when my daughter no longer had passion for cheerleading, we channeled her energy toward her new love, the high school band.

The level of sacrifice only escalated as each of them progressed thru their high school years. One of the most significant was the calculated decision to keep them in their same school even though my new job would require an 80 plus mile, one and one-half hour compute each way. This turned into a six year commuting commitment because our children were born two years apart. When my daughter graduated from high school, my son was only a rising junior.

As each of the children entered college our commitment to purposeful sacrifice ramped up several notches. We raided savings, took out loans and otherwise realigned our finances to ensure that our children received the education essential to their future. We wanted to eliminate most of the distractions that would have hindered their studies like working long hours waiting tables. We provided small allowances to keep change in their pockets.

But more importantly, we encouraged them to build a work ethic and help support themselves by taking on tasks such as being a resident assistant or a student athlete. My daughter earned free room and board for three years while being responsible for hundreds of students many of whom were older than her. Likewise, our son chose to be a year-round student athlete to earn a partial scholarship that grew each year as he excelled at his sport. You cannot imagine how difficult it was to remain on top of his studies and his competition for four solid years. Both of our children took on these tasks without ever complaining.

Chapter 44 - Parting Words of Wisdom

In 1923, some of the most powerful and wealthy financiers met at the Edgewater Beach Hotel in Chicago. They had met to strategize and collaborate together on their personal fortunes as well as to discuss the economies of the civilized world. Among the powerful movers and shakers of the last century who attended this meeting were men who had been or would become:

- the president of the largest independent steel company in the world;
- the president of the New York Stock Exchange;
- a member of the President of the United States cabinet;
- the most successful trader on Wall Street;
- the head of the world's largest industrial monopoly.
- and the president of the Bank of International Settlement.

According to one source, collectively, these men controlled more wealth than there was in the United States Treasury. For years, the newspapers and magazines had been printing their success stories and urged the youth of America to follow their examples.

Eight years after that historic conference in the Edgewater Beach Hotel, in 1931, James Truslow Adams coined a phrase when he delivered a speech during which he encouraged everyone to join in this American Dream . . . the pursuit of gaining status and personal recognition.

This book is not intended to destroy your image of America. It is also not my intent to have you abandon your dreams of success and achieving your goals in what is arguably the greatest country this world has ever seen. Moreover, I do not want you to close this book under the impression that no matter what you do you will always receive the short end of the stick. However, my purpose is to get you to begin thinking critically about the way you have traditionally approached pursuing your dreams. It is my desire that you challenge your previously held assumptions regarding what has either propelled you forward or has made your path difficult or nearly impossible. I hope that you are now more conscious of the economic climate you must toil in every day.

From this day forth, live every day as if your financial life depends on it. Scrutinize every decision that does or will cost you a portion of the wealth you have or will acquire in the years to come. Treat as suspect any offer, proposal or idea that is supposed to make your life better. Keep in mind that anyone who wants to help you reach your American Dream is only trying to get you to help them get one step closer to accomplishing their own dream. This does not mean that every one is out to sham or take advantage of you. However, if a sucker is born every minute, a con artist is born every second!

Also, be willing and ready to make the sacrifices needed to grow that family money tree. Even if that means you may never get to see the fruit grow on the tree, your diligence, discipline and patience will pay off for those grand kids. This not only equates to living financially responsible lives but spending time and effort to teach what you have learned to those that must follow the trails you have blazed. This may also add up to eliminating behaviors and habits that will inevitably leave you withering under the financial heat of this world.

Because of the recent financial events, many Americans have taken a stance on the condition of the American Dream. One camp of people believe that the American Dream is definitely dead. Another camp believes that it is on life support with a very poor prognosis for survival. For these, nothing short of a miracle will make any quality of life possible. That means they are convinced that it will not survive or fully recover. Finally, there are some who staunchly believe that the American Dream is bound to make a full recovery after a substantial period of financial therapy.

As for me, I choose to believe that neither of these concepts are practical or realistic. First, the American Dream can't die because it was never alive! By its very definition, a dream is something that is not based in reality. It is an invention of someone's imagination. In dream mode nothing is impossible. Climbing bare walls, flying without a plane or fighting off a lion with your bare hands are all possible when you are dreaming. However, we can't dream our way through life. We live in a sobering reality that every financial miscalculation can be fatal, every errant purchase makes that desert just a little more arid. Therefore, I urge you to stop banking on a dream or focusing on that mirage of future wealth. Instead, be ready and willing to do whatever it takes to survive in this Desert Land we call America.

By the way, those powerful men mentioned earlier who met at the Edgewater Beach Hotel in 1923 .. all of their lives ended tragically:
- that president of the New York Stock Exchange was caught stealing and ended up in federal prison;
- that member of the President's own cabinet was pardoned from prison so he could die at home;
- that most successful trader on Wall Street took his own life;
- as did the head of the world's largest industrial monopoly; as did the president of the Bank of International Settlement.

    Do you still believe the Hype?

Bibliography

American Fact Finder . (2011, November). Retrieved from http://factfinder.census.gov/servlet/DownloadDataset Servlet?_lang=en

Cook, John T., & Brown, Larry J. (1993). Two Americas: Racial Differences in Child Poverty in the U.S.: A Linear Trend Analysis to the Year 2010. Medford, MA: Tufts University

GMAT Cheating Scandal Illustrates Computerized Testing Vulnerability. (2009,November). FairTest: The National Center for Fair and Opoen Testing. Retrieved from http://fairtest.org/ets-and-test-cheating

High School Grades Better Predictors of College Graduation. (2009,November). FairTest: The National Center for Fair and Open Testing. Retrieved from http://fairtest.org/high-school-grades-better-predictors-college-gradu/

Immigrant Children in the United States are Growing in Number and Facing Substantial Economic Hardship. (2002). New York, NY: National Center for Children in Poverty, Columbia University.

Lewit, Eugene M. (1993). Why is Poverty Increasing Among Children? Future-of-Children. Volume 3. Number 2. Summer/Fall

Mazel, Ella. (1998). "And don't call me a racist!". Lexington, Massachusetts. Argonaut   Press.

Payne, Ruby K.,(2005). a framework for Understanding Poverty. 4th Revised Edition. Highlands, TX. aha! Process, Inc.

Samuelson, Robert J. (1997). The Culture of Poverty. Newsweek. Volume 129. number 18. May 5.

SAT Losing Market-Share To ACT, Test-Optional Colleges. The National Center for Fair and Open Testing. Retrieved from http://fairtest.org/sat-losing-marketshare-act-testoptional-colleges

The Poorest Among Us. (1996). U.S News & World report. Volume 121. Number 25. December 23.

Walters, Ronald W. (2005). White Nationalism Black Interests: Conservative Public Policy and the Black Community.

Zill, Nicholaus. (1993). The Changing Realities of Family Life. Aspen Institute Quarterly, Volume 5. November 1. WInter pp. 27-51.

www.ingramcontent.com/pod-product-compliance
Lightning Source LLC
Chambersburg PA
CBHW020238290526
45784CB00003B/1018